BHAGAVAD GITA

AS VIEWED BY
SWAMI VIVEKANANDA

Compiled by
Swami Madhurananda

Advaita Ashrama
(PUBLICATION DEPARTMENT)
5 DEHI ENTALLY ROAD • KOLKATA 700 014

Published by
Swami Bodhasarananda
Adhyaksha, Advaita Ashrama
Mayavati, Champawat
Uttarakhand, Himalayas 262 524
from its Publication Department, Kolkata
mail@advaitaashrama.org
www.advaitaashrama.org

First edition, November 2009
Second Reprint, January 2012
3M3C

ISBN 978-81-7505-332-8

Typeset in Adobe Caslon Pro and APS-DV-Priyanka

Printed in India at
A.G. Printers
Kolkata 700009

PUBLISHER'S NOTE

We are happy to place before the readers *Bhagavad Gita as Viewed by Swami Vivekananda*. Swami Vivekananda's views on the Gita are scattered throughout *The Complete Works of Swami Vivekananda* published by us in nine volumes. The present book is a compilation of these views carefully accomplished by Swami Madhurananda of Advaita Ashrama. The compiler has classified Swami Vivekananda's comments according to the chapters and verses of the Gita. In consequence, the reader is taken through some of the verses of the Gita along with the Swami's commentary, as it were.

Those references that allude to general aspects of the Gita have been grouped and arranged topic-wise in the "Introduction". Those relating to specific verses of the Gita have been placed under those respective verses. There are few references that do not match with the main body of the work; these have been grouped in the "Appendix". The sources of the Swami's comments have been given at the end of the book in "References". This facilitates the readers interested to proceed with a detailed study of the Swami's views on this subject to access his remarks in their original context. There is also an "Index" at the end, wherein the references to the Gita in *The Complete Works of Swami Vivekananda* have been arranged according to the volumes and pages of the latter. The verses of the Gita have been given in original Devanagari script along with their translations, taken from *Universal Message of Srimad Bhagavad Gita* by Swami Ranganathananda.

The influence of the Gita on other scriptures of the world's religions and systems of thought has been currently accepted and established. Its fascination lies in the humanness of its context as well as its universality of ideas—ideas which have resounded through the ages and come down to our own times. Every discerning reader will find in Swami Vivekananda's speeches and writings the vibrant echoes of the Upanishads and the Bhagavad Gita. And there is no gainsaying that the distinctiveness and originality of his views, laced with his characteristic boldness, are as much intellectually stimulating as they are inspiring.

We are sure the present compilation will prove to be engrossing for all those who are interested in this universal scripture, more so for the students and research scholars of this great subject.

13 August 2009   PUBLISHER

it pass current in the name of his Guru or of someone else. In such cases it is very hazardous for the investigator of historical facts to get at the truth. In ancient times they had no knowledge whatever of geography; imagination ran riot. And so we meet with such fantastic creations of the brain as sweet-ocean, milk-ocean, clarified-butter-ocean, curd-ocean, etc! In the Puranas, we find one living ten thousand years, another a hundred thousand years! But the Vedas say, शतायुर्वै पुरुष:—"Man lives a hundred years." Whom shall we follow here? So, to reach a correct conclusion in the case of Krishna is well-nigh impossible.

It is human nature to build round the real character of a great man all sorts of imaginary superhuman attributes. As regards Krishna the same must have happened, but it seems quite probable that he was a king. Quite probable I say, because in ancient times in our country it was chiefly the kings who exerted themselves most in the preaching of *Brahma-Jnana**. Another point to be especially noted here is that whoever might have been the author of the Gita, we find its teachings the same as those in the whole of the *Mahabharata*. From this we can safely infer that in the age of the *Mahabharata* some great man arose and preached the *Brahma-Jnana* in this new garb to the then existing society. Another fact comes to the fore that in the olden days, as one sect after another arose, there also came into existence and use among them one new scripture or another. It happened, too, that in the lapse of time both the sect and its scripture died out, or the sect ceased to exist but its scripture remained. Similarly, it was quite probable that the Gita was the scripture of such a sect which had embodied its high and noble ideals in this sacred book.

Now to the third point, bearing on the subject of the Kurukshetra War, no special evidence in support of it can be adduced.† But there is no doubt that there was a war fought

---

* Knowledge of the Supreme Reality, Brahman.
† This was true during Swami Vivekananda's time. However, in the first

between the Kurus and the Panchalas. Another thing: how could there be so much discussion about *jnana, bhakti,* and yoga on the battlefield, where the huge army stood in battle array ready to fight, just waiting for the last signal? And was any shorthand writer present there to note down every word spoken between Krishna and Arjuna, in the din and turmoil of the battlefield? According to some, this Kurukshetra War is only an allegory. When we sum up its esoteric significance, it means the war which is constantly going on within man between the tendencies of good and evil. This meaning, too, may not be irrational.

About the fourth point, there is enough ground of doubt as regards the historicity of Arjuna and others, and it is this: *Shatapatha Brahmana* is a very ancient book. In it are mentioned somewhere all the names of those who were the performers of the Ashvamedha Yajna*; but in those places there is not only no mention, but no hint even of the names of Arjuna and others, though it speaks of Janamejaya, the son of Parikshit who was a grandson of Arjuna. Yet in the *Mahabharata* and other books it is stated that Yudhishthira, Arjuna, and others celebrated the Ashvamedha sacrifice.

One thing should be especially remembered here, that there is no connection between these historical researches and our real aim, which is the knowledge that leads to the acquirement of dharma. Even if the historicity of the whole thing is proved to be absolutely false today, it will not in the least be any loss to us. Then what is the use of so much historical research, you may ask. It has its use, because we have to get at the truth; it will not do for us to remain bound by wrong ideas born of ignorance. In this country people think very little of the importance of such

---

decade after India's independence, archeologists excavated a site near Delhi which confirmed the authenticity of the great Kurukshetra War.

* The Vedic horse sacrifice.

inquiries. Many of the sects believe that in order to preach a good thing which may be beneficial to many, there is no harm in telling an untruth, if that helps such preaching, or in other words, the end justifies the means.[1]

Many are of opinion that the Gita was not written at the time of the *Mahabharata*, but was subsequently added to it. This is not correct. The special teachings of the Gita are to be found in every part of the *Mahabharata*, and if the Gita is to be expunged, as forming no part of it, every other portion of it which embodies the same teachings should be similarly treated.[2]

The worship of Shri Krishna is much older than that of Buddha, and if the Gita be not of the same date as the *Mahabharata*, it is surely much earlier and by no means later. The style of language of the Gita is the same as that of the *Mahabharata*. Most of the adjectives used in the Gita to explain matters spiritual are used in the Vana and other Parvans* of the *Mahabharata*, respecting matters temporal. Such coincidence is impossible without the most general and free use of those words at one and the same time. Again, the line of thought in the Gita is the same as in the *Mahabharata*; and when the Gita notices the doctrines of all the religious sects of the time, why does it not ever mention the name of Buddhism?

In spite of the most cautious efforts of the writers subsequent to Buddha, reference to Buddhism is not withheld and appears somewhere or other, in some shape or other, in histories, stories, essays, and every book of the post-Buddhistic literature. In covert or overt ways, some allusion is sure to be met with in reference to Buddha and Buddhism. Can anyone show any such reference in the Gita? Again, the Gita is an attempt at the reconciliation of all religious creeds, none of which is slighted in it. Why, it remains to be answered, is Buddhism alone denied the tender touch of the Gita-writer? The Gita wilfully scorns none. Fear?—Of that

---

* Sections.

there is a conspicuous absence in it. The Lord Himself, being the interpreter and the establisher of the Vedas, never hesitates to even censure Vedic rash presumptuousness if required. Why then should He fear Buddhism?[3]

To understand the Gita requires its historical background. The Gita is a commentary on the Upanishads.[4]

THE GITA AND OTHER SCRIPTURES

The *Bhagavad Gita*—most of you, perhaps, have read it, it is the best commentary we have on the Vedanta philosophy.[5]

The *Bhagavad Gita* is the best authority on Vedanta.[6]

The only commentary, the authoritative commentary on the Vedas, has been made once and for all by Him who inspired the Vedas—by Krishna in the Gita. It is there for every one in every occupation of life.[7]

Than the Gita no better commentary on the Vedas has been written or can be written. The essence of the *shruti*s, or of the Upanishads, is hard to be understood, seeing that there are so many commentators, each one trying to interpret in his own way. Then the Lord Himself comes, He who is the inspirer of the *shruti*s, to show us the meaning of them, as the preacher of the Gita, and today India wants nothing better, the world wants nothing better than that method of interpretation. It is a wonder that subsequent interpreters of the scriptures, even commenting upon the Gita, many times could not catch the meaning, many times could not catch the drift. For what do you find in the Gita, and what in modern commentators? One non-dualistic commentator takes up an Upanishad; there are so many dualistic passages, and he twists and tortures them into some meaning, and wants to bring them all into a meaning of his own. If a dualistic commentator comes, there are so many non-dualistic texts which he begins to torture, to bring them all round to dualistic meaning. But you find in the Gita there is no attempt at torturing any one of them. They are all right, says the Lord; for slowly and gradually the human soul rises up and up, step after step, from the gross to the fine, from the fine to the finer, until it reaches the Absolute, the goal. That is what is in the Gita. Even the *karma-kanda* is taken up, and it is shown that although it cannot give salvation direct, but only indirectly, yet that is also valid; images are valid indirectly; ceremonies, forms, everything is valid only with one condition, purity of the heart.[8]

The Upanishads and the Gita are the true scriptures.[9]

The Gita is the gist of the Vedas. It is not our Bible; the Upanishads are our Bible. It [the Gita] is the gist of the Upanishads and harmonizes the many contradictory parts of the Upanishads.[10]

For the whole gist of the Upanishads was contained in the Gita.[11]

The Gita takes the ideas of the Upanishads and in [some] cases the very words. They are strung together with the idea of bringing out, in a compact, condensed, and systematic form, the whole subject the Upanishads deal with.[12]

Now it is for us to see what there is in the Gita. If we study the Upanishads we notice, in wandering through the mazes of many irrelevant subjects, the sudden introduction of the discussion of a great truth, just as in the midst of a huge wilderness a traveller unexpectedly comes across here and there an exquisitely beautiful rose, with its leaves, thorns, roots, all entangled. Compared with that, the Gita is like these truths beautifully arranged together in their proper places—like a fine garland or a bouquet of the choicest flowers.[13]

In the more recent Upanishads, the spiritual ideas have been collected and brought into one place; as in the *Bhagavad Gita*, for instance, which we may, perhaps, look upon as the last of the Upanishads, you do not find any inkling of these ritualistic ideas. The Gita is like a bouquet composed of beautiful flowers of spiritual truths collected from the Upanishads. But in the Gita you cannot study the rise of the spiritual ideas, you cannot trace them to their source. To do that, as has been pointed out by many, you must study the Vedas.[14]

Then, between the Upanishads and the Sutras,* which are the systematising of the marvellous truths of the Vedanta, comes in the Gita, the divine commentary of the Vedanta. The Upanishads, the *Vyasa-Sutras*, and the Gita, therefore, have been taken up by every sect in India that wants to claim authority for orthodoxy, whether dualist, or Vishishtadvaitist, or Advaitist; the authorities of each of these are the three *prasthanas*.[15]

Either one hears the Advaita-Keshari roaring in peals of thunder—the Asti, Bhati, and Priya[†]—amidst the heart-stopping solemnities of the Himalayan forests, mixing with the solemn cadence of the river of heaven, or listens to the cooing of the Piya, Pitam[‡] in the beautiful bowers of the grove of Vrinda: whether one mingles with the sedate meditations of the monasteries of Varanasi or the ecstatic dances of the followers of the Prophet of Nadia; whether one sits at the feet of the teacher of the Vishishtadvaita system with its Vadakale, Tenkale,[§] and all the other sub-divisions, or listens with reverence to the Acharyas of the Madhva school; whether one hears the martial "Wa Guruki Fateh"[¶] of the secular Sikhs or the sermons on the *Grantha Sahib* of the Udasis and Nirmalas; whether he salutes the *sannyasin* disciples of Kabir with "Sat Sahib" and listens with joy to the Sakhis (bhajans); whether he pores upon the wonderful lore of that reformer of Rajputana, Dadu, or the works of his royal disciple, Sundaradasa, down to the great Nishchaladasa, the celebrated author of *Vichara-sagara*,

---

* *Brahma Sutras*—the aphorisms on Vedanta.
† Existence (Sat), Consciousness (Chit), and Bliss (Ananda)—the three indicatives of Brahman.
‡ A kind of a bird; herein the reference is to the cowherd maids and Krishna.
§ The two divisions of the Ramanuja sect.
¶ Victory to the Guru.

which book has more influence in India than any that has been written in any language within the last three centuries; if even one asks the Bhangi Mehtar of Northern India to sit down and give an account of the teachings of his Lalguru—one will find that all these various teachers and schools have as their basis that system whose authority is the *shruti*, Gita its divine commentary, the *Shariraka-Sutra*s its organized system, and all the different sects in India, from the Paramahamsa Parivrajakacharyas to the poor despised Mehtar disciples of Lalguru, are different manifestations. The three *prasthana*s,* then, in their different explanations as Dvaita, Vishistadvaita, or Advaita, with a few minor recensions, form the "authorities" of the Hindu religion.[16]

The great glory of Shankaracharya was his preaching of the Gita. It is one of the greatest works that this great man did among the many noble works of his noble life—the preaching of the Gita and writing the most beautiful commentary upon it. And he has been followed by all founders of the orthodox sects in India, each of whom has written a commentary on the Gita.[17]

The Hindus visit foreign countries—Rangoon, Java, Hongkong, Madagascar, Suez, Aden, Malta—and they take with them Ganga water and the Gita. The Gita and the sacred waters of the Ganga constitute the Hinduism of the Hindus.[18]

The Gita no doubt has already become the Bible of Hinduism, and it fully deserves to be so.[19]

The Gita is to the Hindus what the *New Testament* is to the Christians.[20]

There are a great many similarities in the teaching of the *New Testament* and the Gita. The human thought goes the same way.[21]

God is everywhere preached in the Gita. Hinduism is nothing without God. The Vedas are nothing without Him.[22]

---

* The three "courses": The Upanishads, the Gita, and the *Brahma Sutra*s, also known as *Shariraka Sutra*s or *Vedanta Sutra*s.

THE GITA AND SHRI KRISHNA

Krishna can never be understood until you have studied the Gita, for he was the embodiment of his own teaching. Every one of these Incarnations came as a living illustration of what they came to preach. Krishna, the preacher of the Gita, was all his life the embodiment of the Song Celestial; he was the great illustration of non-attachment.[23]

With every great Prophet his life is the only commentary. Look at his life: what he did will bear out the texts. Read the Gita, and you will find that is exactly borne out by the life of the Teacher.[24]

Shri Krishna spoke the Gita, establishing Himself in the Atman. Those passages of the Gita where He speaks with the word "I", invariably indicate the Atman: "Take refuge in Me alone" means, "Be established in the Atman". This knowledge of the Atman is the highest aim of the Gita. The references to yoga etc. are but incidental to this realization of the Atman. Those who have not this knowledge of the Atman are "suicides". "They kill themselves by the clinging to the unreal"; they lose their life in the noose of sense-pleasures. You are also men, and can't you ignore this trash of sensual enjoyment that won't last for two days? Should you also swell the ranks of those who are born and die in utter ignorance? Accept the "beneficial" and discard the "pleasant". Speak of this Atman to all, even to the lowest. By continued speaking your own intelligence also will clear up. And always repeat the great *mantra*s "तत्त्वमसि—Thou art That", "सोऽहमस्मि—I am That", "सर्वं खल्विदं ब्रह्म—All this is verily Brahman"—and have the courage of a lion in the heart. What is there to fear? Fear is death—fear is the greatest sin. The human soul, represented by Arjuna, was touched with fear. Therefore Bhagavan Shri Krishna, established in the Atman, spoke to him the teachings of the Gita. Still his fear would not leave him. Later, when Arjuna saw the Universal Form of the Lord, and became established in the Atman, then with all bondages of karma burnt by the fire of knowledge, he fought the battle.[25]

Now from His playful life at Vrindavan come to the Krishna of Kurukshetra, and see how that also is fascinating—how, amidst all that horrible din and uproar of fighting, Krishna remains calm, balanced, and peaceful. Ay, on the very battlefield, He is speaking the Gita to Arjuna and getting him on to fight, which is the dharma of a *kshatriya**! Himself an agent to bring about this terrible warfare, Shri Krishna remains unattached to action—He did not take up arms! To whichsoever phase of it you look, you will find the character of Shri Krishna perfect. As if He was the embodiment of knowledge, work, devotion, power of concentration, and everything! In the present age, this aspect of Shri Krishna should be specially studied. Only contemplating the Krishna of Vrindavan with His flute won't do nowadays—that will not bring salvation to humanity. Now is needed the worship of Shri Krishna uttering forth the lion-roar of the Gita, of Rama with His bow and arrows, of Mahavira, of Mother Kali. Then only will the people grow strong by going to work with great energy and will.[26]

Keep aside for the present the Vrindavan aspect of Shri Krishna, and spread far and wide the worship of Shri Krishna roaring the Gita out, with the voice of a lion. And bring into daily use the worship of Shakti—the divine Mother, the source of all power.[27]

A SOURCE OF STRENGTH

The Gita—"that wonderful poem, without one note in it of weakness or unmanliness."[28]

First of all, our young men must be strong. Religion will come afterwards. Be strong, my young friends; that is my advice to you.

---

* The caste of warriors in the Hindu society.

You will be nearer to Heaven through football than through the study of the Gita. These are bold words; but I have to say them, for I love you. I know where the shoe pinches. I have gained a little experience. You will understand the Gita better with your biceps, your muscles, a little stronger. You will understand the mighty genius and the mighty strength of Krishna better with a little of strong blood in you.[29]

Now it won't do to merely quote the authority of our ancient books. The tidal wave of Western civilization is now rushing over the length and breadth of the country. It won't do now simply to sit in meditation on mountain tops without realizing in the least its usefulness. Now is wanted—as said in the Gita by the Lord— intense *karma-yoga*, with unbounded courage and indomitable strength in the heart. Then only will the people of the country be roused, otherwise they will continue to be as much in the dark as you are.[30]

"Ought one to seek an opportunity of death in defence of right, or ought one to take the lesson of the Gita and learn never to react?" the Swami was asked. "I am for no reaction", said the Swami, speaking slowly and with a long pause. Then he added "—for *sannyasins*. Self-defence for the householder!"[31]

[The following paragraph is Sister Nivedita's notes of a New York Bhagavad Gita class, recorded in a June 16, 1900 letter to Miss Josephine MacLeod.]

"This morning the lesson on the Gita was grand. It began with a long talk on the fact that the highest ideals are not for all. Nonresistance is not for the man who thinks the replacing of the maggot in the wound by the leprous saint with 'Eat, Brother!' disgusting and horrible. Nonresistance is practised by a mother's love towards an angry child. It is a travesty in the mouth of a coward, or in the face of a lion."[32]

THE GENERAL TEACHINGS OF THE GITA

The reconciliation of the different paths of dharma, and work without desire or attachment—these are the two special characteristics of the Gita.[33]

In Krishna we find ... two ideas [stand] supreme in his message: The first is the harmony of different ideas; the second is non-attachment. A man can attain to perfection, the highest goal, sitting on a throne, commanding armies, working out big plans for nations. In fact, Krishna's great sermon was preached on the battlefield.[34]

a) *Harmony of Paths*

Of the different philosophies, the tendency of the Hindu is not to destroy, but to harmonize everything. If any new idea comes into India, we do not antagonize it, but simply try to take it in, to harmonize it, because this method was taught first by our prophet, God incarnate on earth, Shri Krishna. This Incarnation of God preached himself first: "I am the God Incarnate, I am the inspirer of all books, I am the inspirer of all religions." Thus we do not reject any.[35]

Now let us see some of the main points discussed in the Gita. Wherein lies the originality of the Gita which distinguishes it from all preceding scriptures? It is this: Though before its advent, yoga, *jnana*, *bhakti*, etc. had each its strong adherents, they all quarrelled among themselves, each claiming superiority for its own chosen path; no one ever tried to seek for reconciliation among these different paths. It was the author of the Gita who for the first time tried to harmonize these. He took the best from what all the sects then existing had to offer and threaded them in the Gita. But even where Krishna failed to show a complete reconciliation (*samanvaya*) among these warring sects, it was fully accomplished by Ramakrishna Paramahamsa in this nineteenth century. ... The reconciliation of the different paths of dharma, and work without desire or attachment—these are the two special characteristics of the Gita.[36]

When the Gita was first preached, there was then going on a great controversy between two sects. One party considered the Vedic *yajna*s and animal sacrifices and such like karmas to constitute the whole of religion. The other preached that the killing of numberless horses and cattle cannot be called religion. The people belonging to the latter party were mostly *sannyasin*s and followers of *jnana*. They believed that the giving up of all work and the gaining of the knowledge of the Self was the only path to *moksha*. By the preaching of His great doctrine of work without motive, the Author of the Gita set at rest the disputes of these two antagonistic sects.[37]

Ancient India had for centuries been the battlefield for the ambitious projects of two of her foremost classes—the *brahmin*s and the *kshatriya*s. On the one hand, the priesthood stood between the lawless social tyranny of the princes over the masses, whom the *kshatriya*s declared to be their legal food. On the other hand, the *kshatriya* power was the one potent force which struggled with any success against the spiritual tyranny of the priesthood and the ever-increasing chain of ceremonials which they were forging to bind down the people with. The tug of war began in the earliest periods of the history of our race, and throughout the *shruti*s it can be distinctly traced. A momentary lull came when Shri Krishna, leading the faction of *kshatriya* power and of *jnana*, showed the way to reconciliation. The result was the teachings of the Gita—the essence of philosophy, of liberality, of religion. Yet the causes were there, and the effect must follow.[38]

On the one hand, the majority of the priests impelled by economical considerations were bound to defend that form of religion which made their existence a necessity of society and assigned them the highest place in the scale of caste; on the other hand, the king-caste, whose strong right hand guarded and guided the nation and who now found itself as leading in the higher thoughts also, were loath to give up the first place to men who only knew how to conduct a ceremonial. There were then others, recruited from both the priests and king-castes, who ridiculed equally the ritualists and philosophers, declared spiritualism as fraud and priestcraft, and upheld the attainment of material comforts as the highest goal of life. The people, tired of ceremonials and wondering at the philosophers, joined in masses the materialists. This was the beginning of that caste question and that triangular fight in India between ceremonials, philosophy, and materialism which has come down unsolved to our own days. The first solution of the difficulty attempted was by applying the eclecticism which from the earliest days had taught the people to see in differences the same truth in various garbs. The great leader of this school, Krishna—himself of royal race—and his sermon, the Gita, have after various vicissitudes, brought about by the upheavals of the Jains, the Buddhists, and other sects, fairly established themselves as the "Prophet" of India and the truest philosophy of life. Though the tension was toned down for the time, it did not satisfy the social wants which were among the causes—the claim of the king-race to stand first in the scale of caste and the popular intolerance of priestly privilege. Krishna had opened the gates of spiritual knowledge and attainment to all irrespective of sex or caste, but he left undisturbed the same problem on the social side.[39]

So the great struggle began in India and it comes to one of its culminating points in the Gita. When it was causing fear that all India was going to be broken up between [the] two ... [groups], there rose this man Krishna, and in the Gita he tries to reconcile the ceremony and the philosophy of the priests and the people.[40]

In the Gita the way is laid open to all men and women, to all caste and colour.[41]

b.) *Nishkama Karma*

You who have read the Gita see all through the book that the one idea is non-attachment. Remain unattached.[42]

Now let us see some of the main points discussed in the Gita. ... The next is, *nishkama karma,* or work without desire or attachment. People nowadays understand what is meant by this in various ways. Some say what is implied by being unattached is to become purposeless. If that were its real meaning, then heartless brutes and the walls would be the best exponents of the performance of *nishkama karma.* Many others, again, give the example of Janaka, and wish themselves to be equally recognized as past masters in the practice of *nishkama karma!* Janaka (lit. father) did not acquire that distinction by bringing forth children, but these people all want to be Janakas, with the sole qualification of being the fathers of a brood of children! No! The true *nishkama karmi* (performer of work without desire) is neither to be like a brute, nor to be inert, nor heartless. He is not *tamasika* but of pure *sattva.* His heart is so full of love and sympathy that he can embrace the whole world with his love. The world at large cannot generally comprehend his all-embracing love and sympathy.[43]

Now, what is the meaning of working without motive? Nowadays many understand it in the sense that one is to work in such a way that neither pleasure nor pain touches his mind. If this be its real meaning, then the animals might be said to work without motive. Some animals devour their own offspring, and they do not feel any pangs at all in doing so. Robbers ruin other people by robbing them of their possessions; but if they feel quite callous to pleasure or pain, then they also would be working without motive. If the meaning of it be such, then one who has a stony heart, the worst of criminals, might be considered to be working without motive. The walls have no feelings of pleasure or pain, neither has a stone, and it cannot be said that they are working without motive. In the above sense the doctrine is a potent instrument in the hands of the wicked. They would go on doing wicked deeds, and would pronounce themselves as working without a motive. If such be the significance of working without a motive, then a fearful doctrine has been put forth by the preaching of the Gita. Certainly this is not the meaning. Furthermore, if we look into the lives of those who were connected with the preaching of the Gita, we should find them living quite a different life. Arjuna killed Bhishma and Drona in battle, but withal, he sacrificed all his self-interest and desires and his lower self millions of times.

Gita teaches *karma-yoga*. We should work through yoga (concentration). In such concentration in action (*karma-yoga*), there is no consciousness of the lower ego present. The consciousness that I am doing this and that is never present when one works through yoga. The Western people do not understand this. They say that if there be no consciousness of ego, if this ego is gone, how then can a man work? But when one works with concentration, losing all consciousness of oneself, the work that is done will be infinitely better, and this every one may have experienced in his own life. We perform many works subconsciously, such as the digestion of food etc., many others consciously, and others again by becoming immersed in *samadhi* as it were, when there is no consciousness of the smaller ego. If the painter, losing the consciousness of his ego, becomes completely immersed in his painting, he will be able to produce masterpieces. The good cook concentrates his whole self on the food-material he handles; he loses all other consciousness for the time being. But they are only able to do perfectly a single work in this way, to which they are habituated. The Gita teaches that all works should be done thus. He who is one with the Lord through yoga performs all his works by becoming immersed in concentration, and does not seek any personal benefit. Such a performance of work brings only good to the world, no evil can come out of it. Those who work thus never do anything for themselves.[44]

We say that we cannot do good without at the same time doing some evil, or do evil without doing some good. Knowing this, how can we work? There have, therefore, been sects in this world who have in an astoundingly preposterous way preached slow suicide as the only means to get out of the world, because if a man lives, he has to kill poor little animals and plants or do injury to something or some one. So according to them the only way out of the world is to die. The Jains have preached this doctrine as their highest ideal. This teaching seems to be very logical. But the true solution is found in the Gita. It is the theory of non-attachment, to be attached to nothing while doing our work of life. Know that you are separated entirely from the world, though you are in the world, and that whatever you may be doing in it, you are not doing that for your own sake.[45]

For in the Gita Shri Krishna says—men should work for work's sake only, and love for love's sake.[46]

c) *Bhakti*

The Upanishads deal elaborately with *shraddha* in many places, but hardly mention *bhakti*. In the Gita, on the other hand, the subject of *bhakti* is not only again and again dealt with, but in it, the innate spirit of *bhakti* has attained its culmination.[47]

If you want to be a *bhakta*, it is not at all necessary for you to know whether Krishna was born in Mathura or in Vraja, what he was doing, or just the exact date on which he pronounced the teachings of the Gita. You only require to feel the craving for the beautiful lessons of duty and love in the Gita. All the other particulars about it and its author are for the enjoyment of the learned.[48]

So says Krishna in the Gita: The Lord is the only One who never changes. His love never fails. Wherever we are and whatever we do, He is ever and ever the same merciful, the same loving heart. He never changes, He is never angry, whatever we do. How can God be angry with us? Your babe does many mischievous things: are you angry with that babe? Does not God know what we are going to be? He knows we are all going to be perfect, sooner or later. He has patience, infinite patience. We must love Him, and everyone that lives—only in and through Him. This is the keynote.[49]

To obtain *bhakti*, seek the company of holy men who have *bhakti*, and read books like the Gita and *The Imitation of Christ*; always think of the attributes of God.[50]

d) *Jnana*

Jnana is taught very clearly by Krishna in the *Bhagavad-Gita*. This great poem is held to be the Crown jewel of all Indian literature. It is a kind of commentary on the Vedas. It shows us that our battle for spirituality must be fought out in this life; so we must not flee from it, but rather compel it to give us all that it holds. As the Gita typifies this struggle for higher things, it is highly poetical to lay the scene in a battlefield. Krishna in the guise of a charioteer to Arjuna, leader of one of the opposing armies, urges him not to be sorrowful, not to fear death, since he knows he is immortal, that nothing which changes can be in the real nature of man. Through chapter after chapter, Krishna teaches the higher truths of philosophy and religion to Arjuna. It is these teachings which make this poem so wonderful; practically the whole of the Vedanta philosophy is included in them.[51]

Krishna, the "Lord of souls", talks to Arjuna or Gudakesha, "lord of sleep" (he who has conquered sleep). The "field of virtue" (the battlefield) is this world; the five brothers (representing righteousness) fight the hundred other brothers (all that we love and have to contend against); the most heroic brother, Arjuna (the awakened soul), is the general. We have to fight all sense-delights, the things to which we are most attached, to kill them.

We have to stand alone; we are Brahman, all other ideas must be merged in this one.[52]

Wisdom can be practised even on a battlefield. The Gita was preached so.[53]

THE GREATNESS AND INFLUENCE OF THE GITA

The greatest incident of the war was the marvellous and immortal poem of the Gita, the Song Celestial. It is the popular scripture of India and the loftiest of all teachings. It consists of a dialogue held by Arjuna with Krishna, just before the commencement of the fight on the battlefield of Kurukshetra. I would advise those of you who have not read that book to read it. If you only knew how much it has influenced your own country even! If you want to know the source of Emerson's inspiration, it is this book, the Gita. He went to see Carlyle, and Carlyle made him a present of the Gita; and that little book is responsible for the Concord Movement. All the broad movements in America, in one way or other, are indebted to the Concord party.[54]

First see the irony of it. Jesus Christ, the God of the Europeans, has taught: Have no enemy, bless them that curse you; whosoever shall smite thee on thy right cheek, turn to him the other also; stop all your work and be ready for the next world; the end of the world is near at hand. And our Lord in the Gita is saying: Always work with great enthusiasm, destroy your enemies and enjoy the world. But, after all, it turned out to be exactly the reverse of what Christ or Krishna implied. The Europeans never took the words of Jesus Christ seriously. Always of active habits, being possessed of a tremendous *rajasika* nature, they are gathering with great enterprise and youthful ardour the comforts and luxuries of the different countries of the world and enjoying them to their hearts' content. And we are sitting in a corner, with our bag and baggage, pondering on death day and night, and singing, "नलिनीदलगतजलमतितरलं तद्वज्जीवनमतिशयचपलम्—Very tremulous and unsteady is the water on the lotus-leaf; so is the life of man frail and transient"—with the result that it is making our blood run cold and our flesh creep with the fear of Yama, the god of death; and Yama, too, alas, has taken us at our word, as it were— plague and all sorts of maladies have entered into our country! Who are following the teachings of the Gita?—the Europeans. And who are acting according to the will of Jesus Christ?—The descendants of Shri Krishna![55]

Take the Sermon on the Mount and the Gita—they are simplicity itself. Even the streetwalker can understand them. How grand! In them you find the truth clearly and simply revealed.[56]

The restless Western atheist or agnostic finds in the Gita or in the *Dhammapada* the only place where his soul can anchor.[57]

As a character Buddha was the greatest the world has ever seen; next to him Christ. But the teachings of Krishna as taught by the Gita are the grandest the world has ever known. He who wrote that wonderful poem was one of those rare souls whose lives sent a wave of regeneration through the world. The human race will never again see such a brain as his who wrote the Gita.[58]

Well, now great things are to be done! Who cares for great things? Why not do small things as well? One is as good as the other. The greatness of little things, that is what the Gita teaches—bless the old book![59]

The less you read, the better. Read the Gita and other good works on Vedanta. That is all you need.[60]*

---

* For further information regarding the historical background of the Gita, a general view of the Upanishads, the Vedas, and Shri Krishna, see: "The Gita I" (*The Complete Works of Swami Vivekananda*, 1.446- 58) and "The Mahabharata" (Ibid. 4.78-101). For more details on the philosophical background of the Gita, see: "The Gita" (Ibid. 9.274-76), "The Gita I" (Ibid. 9.276-78) and "Krishna" (Ibid. 1.437-45). For free interpretations of the teachings of the Gita by Swami Vivekananda, see: "The Gita I", "The Gita III" and "Gita Class" (Ibid. 9.276-82).

BHAGAVAD GITA

CHAPTER I

The Gita requires a little preliminary introduction. The scene is laid on the battlefield of Kurukshetra. There were two branches of the same race fighting for the empire of India about five thousand years ago. The Pandavas had the right, but the Kauravas had the might. The Pandavas were five brothers, and they were living in a forest. Krishna was the friend of the Pandavas. The Kauravas would not grant them as much land as would cover the point of a needle. The opening scene is the battlefield, and both sides see their relatives and friends—one brother on one side and another on the other side; a grandfather on one side, grandson on the other side. ... When Arjuna sees his own friends and relatives on the other side and knows that he may have to kill them, his heart gives way and he says that he will not fight. Thus begins the Gita.[1]

The first discourse in the Gita can be taken allegorically.[2]

CHAPTER II

सञ्जय उवाच –
Sanjaya said:

तं तथा कृपयाविष्टमश्रुपूर्णाकुलेक्षणम् ।
विषीदन्तमिदं वाक्यमुवाच मधुसूदनः ॥ १ ॥

To him who was thus overwhelmed with pity and sorrowing, and whose eyes were dimmed with tears, Madhusudana spoke these words. —2. 1

श्रीभगवानुवाच –
The Blessed Lord said:

कुतस्त्वा कश्मलमिदं विषमे समुपस्थितम् ।
अनार्यजुष्टमस्वर्ग्यमकीर्तिकरमर्जुन ॥२॥

In such a strait, whence comes upon thee, O Arjuna, this dejection, un-Aryan-like, disgraceful, and contrary to the attainment of heaven? —2. 2

क्लैब्यं मा स्म गमः पार्थ नैतत् त्वयि उपपद्यते ।
क्षुद्रं हृदयदौर्बल्यं त्यक्त्वोत्तिष्ठ परंतप ॥३॥

Yield not to unmanliness, O son of Pritha! Ill doth it become thee. Cast off this mean faint-heartedness and arise, O scorcher of thine enemies! —2. 3

In the *shloka*s beginning with तं तथा कृपयाविष्टं, how poetically, how beautifully, has Arjuna's real position been painted! Then Shri Krishna advises Arjuna; and in the words क्लैब्यं मा स्म गमः पार्थ etc., why is he goading Arjuna to fight? Because it was not that the disinclination of Arjuna to fight arose out of the overwhelming predominance of pure *sattva guna*; it was all *tamas* that brought on this unwillingness. The nature of a man of *sattva guna* is that he is equally calm in all situations in life—whether it be prosperity or adversity. But Arjuna was afraid, he was overwhelmed with pity. That he had the instinct and the inclination to fight is proved by the simple fact that he came to the battlefield with no other purpose than that. Frequently in our lives also such things are seen to happen. Many people think they are *sattvika* by nature, but they are really nothing but *tamasika*. Many living in an uncleanly way regard themselves as *paramahamsas*! Why? Because the *shastras* say that *paramahamsas* live like one inert, or mad, or like an unclean spirit. *Paramahamsas* are compared to children, but here it should be understood that the comparison is one-sided. The *paramahamsa* and the child are not one and non-different. They only appear similar, being the two extreme poles, as it were. One has reached to a state beyond *jnana*, and the other has not got even an inkling of *jnana*. The quickest and gentlest vibrations of light are both beyond the reach of our ordinary vision; but in the one it is intense heat, and in the other it may be said to be almost without any heat. So it is with the opposite qualities of *sattva* and *tamas*. They seem in some respects to be the same, no doubt, but there is a world of difference between them. The *tamoguna* loves very much to array itself in the garb of the *sattva*. Here, in Arjuna, the mighty warrior, it has come under the guise of *daya* (pity).

In order to remove this delusion which had overtaken Arjuna, what did the Bhagavan say? As I always preach that you should not decry a man by calling him a sinner, but that you should draw his attention to the omnipotent power that is in him, in the same way does the Bhagavan speak to Arjuna. नैतत् त्वयि उपपद्यते—"It doth not befit thee!" "Thou art Atman imperishable, beyond all evil. Having forgotten thy real nature, thou hast, by thinking thyself a sinner, as one afflicted with bodily evils and mental grief, thou hast made thyself so—this doth not befit thee!"—so says the

Bhagavan: "क्लैब्यं मा स्म गमः पार्थ—Yield not to unmanliness, O son of Pritha. There is in the world neither sin nor misery, neither disease nor grief; if there is anything in the world which can be called sin, it is this—'fear'; know that any work which brings out the latent power in thee is *punya* (virtue); and that which makes thy body and mind weak is, verily, sin. Shake off this weakness, this faint-heartedness! क्लैब्यं मा स्म गमः पार्थ—Thou art a hero, a *vira*; this is unbecoming of thee."

If you, my sons, can proclaim this message to the world— क्लैब्यं मा स्म गमः पार्थ—then all this disease, grief, sin, and sorrow will vanish from off the face of the earth in three days. All these ideas of weakness will be nowhere. Now it is everywhere—this current of the vibration of fear. Reverse the current; bring in the opposite vibration, and behold the magic transformation! Thou art omnipotent—go, go to the mouth of the cannon, fear not. Hate not the most abject sinner, look not to his exterior. Turn thy gaze inward, where resides the *paramatman*. Proclaim to the whole world with trumpet voice, "There is no sin in thee, there is no misery in thee; thou art the reservoir of omnipotent power. Arise, awake, and manifest the Divinity within!"

If one reads this one *shloka*—क्लैब्यं मा स्म गमः पार्थ नैतत् त्वयि उपपद्यते। क्षुद्रं हृदयदौर्बल्यं त्यक्त्वोत्तिष्ठ परन्तप ।—one gets all the merits of reading the entire Gita; for in this one *shloka* lies imbedded the whole Message of the Gita.[1]

—"Yield not to unmanliness, O son of Pritha! Ill doth it befit thee. Cast off this mean faint-heartedness and arise, O scorcher of thine enemies." ... In these and similar passages in the Gita the Lord is showing the way to dharma.[2]

For all of us in this world life is a continuous fight. ... Many a time comes when we want to interpret our weakness and cowardice as forgiveness and renunciation. There is no merit in the renunciation of a beggar. If a person who can [give a blow] forbears, there is merit in that. If a person who has, gives up, there is merit in that. We know how often in our lives through laziness and cowardice we give up the battle and try to hypnotize our minds into the belief that we are brave. The Gita opens with this very significant verse: "Arise, O Prince! Give up this faint-heartedness, this weakness! Stand up and fight!" Then Arjuna, trying to argue the matter [with Krishna], brings higher moral ideas, how non-resistance is better than resistance, and so on. He is trying to justify himself, but he cannot fool Krishna. Krishna is the higher Self, or God. He sees through the argument at once. In this case [the motive] is weakness. Arjuna sees his own relatives and he cannot strike them. ... There is a conflict in Arjuna's heart between his emotionalism and his duty. The nearer we are to [beasts and] birds, the more we are in the hells of emotion. We call it love. It is self-hypnotization. We are under the control of our [emotions] like animals. A cow can sacrifice its life for its young. Every animal can. What of that? It is not the blind, birdlike emotion that leads to perfection. ... [To reach] the eternal consciousness, that is the goal of man! There emotion has no place, nor sentimentalism, nor anything that belongs to the senses—only the light of pure reason. [There] man stands as spirit.[3]

In reading the *Bhagavad Gita*, many of you in Western countries may have felt astonished at the second chapter, wherein Shri Krishna calls Arjuna a hypocrite and a coward because of his refusal to fight, or offer resistance, on account of his adversaries being his friends and relatives, making the plea that non-resistance was the highest ideal of love. This is a great lesson for us all to learn, that in all matters the two extremes are alike. The extreme positive and the extreme negative are always similar. When the vibrations of light are too slow, we do not see them, nor do we see them when they are too rapid. So with sound; when very low in pitch, we do not hear it; when very high, we do not hear it either. Of like nature is the difference between resistance and non-resistance. One man does not resist because he is weak, lazy, and cannot, not because he will not; the other man knows that he can strike an irresistible blow if he likes; yet he not only does not strike, but blesses his enemies. The one who from weakness resists not commits a sin, and as such cannot receive any benefit from the non-resistance; while the other would commit a sin by offering resistance. Buddha gave up his throne and renounced his position, that was true renunciation; but there cannot be any question of renunciation in the case of a beggar who has nothing to renounce. So we must always be careful about what we really mean when we speak of this non-resistance and ideal love. We must first take care to understand whether we have the power of resistance or not. Then, having the power, if we renounce it and do not resist, we are doing a grand act of love; but if we cannot resist, and yet, at the same time, try to deceive ourselves into the belief that we are actuated by motives of the highest love, we are doing the exact opposite. Arjuna became a coward at the sight of the mighty array against him; his "love" made him forget his duty towards his country and king. That is why Shri Krishna told him that he was a hypocrite: Thou talkest like a wise man, but thy actions betray thee to be a coward; therefore stand up and fight![4]

And mark you, those things which you see in pusillanimous, effeminate folk who speak in a nasal tone chewing every syllable, whose voice is as thin as of one who has been starving for a week, who are like a tattered wet rag, who never protest or are moved even if kicked by anybody—those are the signs of the lowest *tamas*, those are the signs of death, not of *sattva*—all corruption and stench. It is because Arjuna was going to fall into the ranks of these men that the Lord is explaining matters to him so elaborately in the Gita. Is that not the fact? Listen to the very first words that came out of the mouth of the Lord, "क्लैब्यं मा स्म गमः पार्थ नैतत् त्वयि उपपद्यते—Yield not to unmanliness, O Partha! Ill doth it befit thee!" and then later, "तस्मात्त्वमुत्तिष्ठ यशो लभस्व—Therefore do thou arise and acquire fame." Coming under the influence of the Jains, Buddhas, and others, we have joined the lines of those *tamasika* people. During these last thousand years, the whole country is filling the air with the name of the Lord and is sending its prayers to Him; and the Lord is never lending His ears to them. And why should He? When even man never hears the cries of the fool, do you think God will? Now the only way out is to listen to the words of the Lord in the Gita, "क्लैब्यं मा स्म गमः पार्थ नैतत् त्वयि उपपद्यते—Yield not to unmanliness, O Partha!" "तस्मात्त्वमुत्तिष्ठ यशो लभस्व—Therefore do thou arise and acquire fame."[5]

अशोच्यान् अन्वशोचस्त्वं प्रज्ञावादांश्च भाषसे ।
गतासून् अगतासूंश्च नानुशोचन्ति पण्डिताः ॥११॥

Thou hast been mourning for them who should not be mourned for. Yet thou speakest words of wisdom. The (truly) wise grieve neither for the living nor the dead. —2. 11

There is a conflict in Arjuna's heart between his emotionalism and his duty. The nearer we are to [beasts and] birds, the more we are in the hells of emotion. We call it love. It is self-hypnotization. We are under the control of our [emotions] like animals. A cow can sacrifice its life for its young. Every animal can. What of that? It is not the blind, birdlike emotion that leads to perfection. ... [To reach] the eternal consciousness, that is the goal of man! There emotion has no place, nor sentimentalism, nor anything that belongs to the senses—only the light of pure reason. [There] man stands as spirit. Now, Arjuna is under the control of this emotionalism. He is not what he should be—a great self-controlled, enlightened sage working through the eternal light of reason. He has become like an animal, like a baby, just letting his heart carry away his brain, making a fool of himself and trying to cover his weakness with the flowery names of "love" and so on. Krishna sees through that. Arjuna talks like a man of little learning and brings out many reasons, but at the same time he talks the language of a fool. "The sage is not sorry for those that are living nor for those that die."[6]

Even forgiveness, if weak and passive, is not true: fight is better. Forgive when you could bring legions of angels to the victory. Krishna, the charioteer of Arjuna, hears him say, "Let us forgive our enemies", and answers, "You speak the words of wise men, but you are not a wise man, but a coward". As a lotus-leaf, living in the water yet untouched by it, so should the soul be in the world. This is a battlefield, fight your way out. Life in this world is an attempt to see God. Make your life a manifestation of will strengthened by renunciation.[7]

न त्वेवाहं जातु नासं न त्वं नेमे जनाधिपाः।
न चैव न भविष्यामः सर्वे वयमतः परम् ॥१२॥

Neither myself, nor yourself, nor these kings have been not; and never shall we all cease to be. We are always there even after the death of the body. —2. 12

"You cannot die nor can I. There was never a time when we did not exist. There will never be a time when we shall not exist.[8]

People talk about the beginning of the world, the beginning of man. The word beginning simply means the beginning of the cycle. It nowhere means the beginning of the whole Cosmos. It is impossible that creation could have a beginning. No one of you can imagine a time of beginning. That which has a beginning must have an end. "Never did I not exist, nor you, nor will any of us ever hereafter cease to be," says the *Bhagavad Gita*. Wherever the beginning of creation is mentioned, it means the beginning of a cycle. Your body will meet with death, but your soul, never.[9]

देहिनोऽस्मिन् यथा देहे कौमारं यौवनं जरा।
तथा देहान्तरप्राप्तिः धीरस्तत्र न मुह्यति ॥१३॥

Every embodied person passes through the states of childhood, youth, and old age in the body; similarly also death and rebirth; a courageous person in not deluded thereby. —2. 13

मात्रास्पर्शास्तु कौन्तेय शीतोष्णसुखदुःखदाः ।
आगमापायिनोऽनित्याः तांस्तितिक्षस्व भारत ॥१४॥

Notions of heat and cold, of pain and pleasure, are born, O son
of Kunti, only of the contact of the senses with their objects.
They have a beginning and an end. They are impermanent in
their nature. Bear them patiently, O descendant of Bharata.
—2. 14

यं हि न व्यथयन्त्येते पुरुषं पुरुषर्षभ ।
समदुःखसुखं धीरं सोऽमृतत्वाय कल्पते ॥१५॥

That calm man who is the same in pain and pleasure, whom
these cannot disturb, alone is able, O great amongst men, to
attain to immortality. —2. 15

नासतो विद्यते भावो नाभावो विद्यते सतः ।
उभयोरपि दृष्टोऽन्तः त्वनयोस्तत्त्वदर्शिभिः ॥१६॥

The unreal never is. The Real never is not. Men possessed of
the knowledge of the Truth fully know both these. —2. 16

अविनाशि तु तद्विद्धि येन सर्वमिदं ततम् ।
विनाशमव्ययस्यास्य न कश्चित्कर्तुमर्हति ॥१७॥

Consider that which pervades the whole universe as indestructible; nothing can destroy that inexhaustible reality. —2. 17

अन्तवन्त इमे देहा नित्यस्योक्ताः शरीरिणः ।
अनाशिनोऽप्रमेयस्य तस्मात् युध्यस्व भारत ॥१८॥

These bodies—of the eternal embodied one which is
indestructible and indeterminable—have an end, it is said;
therefore fight, O Arjuna. —2. 18

"As in this life a man begins with childhood, and [passes
through youth and old age, so at death he merely passes into
another kind of body]. Why should a wise man be sorry?" And
where is the beginning of this emotionalism that has got hold of

you? It is in the senses. "It is the touch of the senses that brings all this quality of existence: heat and cold, pleasure and pain. They come and go." Man is miserable this moment, happy the next. As such he cannot experience the nature of the soul.

"Existence can never be non-existence, neither can non-existence ever become existence. ... Know, therefore, that that which pervades all this universe is without beginning or end. It is unchangeable. There is nothing in the universe that can change [the Changeless]. Though this body has its beginning and end, the dweller in the body is infinite and without end."

Knowing this, stand up and fight! Not one step back, that is the idea. ... Fight it out, whatever comes. Let the stars move from the sphere! Let the whole world stand against us! Death means only a change of garment. What of it? Thus fight! You gain nothing by becoming cowards. ... Taking a step backward, you do not avoid any misfortune. You have cried to all the gods in the world. Has misery ceased? The masses in India cry to sixty million gods, and still die like dogs. Where are these gods? ... The gods come to help you when you have succeeded. So what is the use? Die game. ... This bending the knee to superstitions, this selling yourself to your own mind does not befit you, my soul. You are infinite, deathless, birthless. Because you are infinite spirit, it does not befit you to be a slave. ... Arise! Awake! Stand up and fight! Die if you must. There is none to help you. You are all the world. Who can help you?[10]

य एनं वेत्ति हन्तारं यश्चैनं मन्यते हतम् ।
उभौ तौ न विजानीतो नायं हन्ति न हन्यते ॥१९॥

Who considers the Atman as the slayer and who considers this Atman as the slain, both of them do not know that It does not kill nor is It killed. —2. 19

Any action that you do for yourself will bring its effect to bear upon you. If it is a good action, you will have to take the good effect, and if bad, you will have to take the bad effect; but any action that is not done for your own sake, whatever it be, will have no effect on you. There is to be found a very expressive sentence in our scriptures embodying this idea: "Even if he kills the whole universe (or be himself killed), he is neither the killer nor the killed, when he knows that he is not acting for himself at all." Therefore *karma-yoga* teaches, "Do not give up the world; live in the world, imbibe its influences as much as you can; but if it be for your own enjoyment's sake, work not at all." Enjoyment should not be the goal.[11]

न जायते म्रियते वा कदाचित् नायं भूत्वाऽभविता वा न भूयः।
अजो नित्यः शाश्वतोऽयं पुराणो न हन्यते हन्यमाने शरीरे ॥२०॥

This Self is never born nor does It ever die; it is not something that having been born, It again ceases to be; unborn, eternal, and everlasting, this ancient One is not killed when the body is killed. —2. 20

Now freedom is only possible when no external power can exert any influence, produce any change. Freedom is only possible to the being who is beyond all conditions, all laws, all bondages of cause and effect. In other words, the unchangeable alone can be free and, therefore, immortal. This Being, this Atman, this real Self of man, the free, the unchangeable is beyond all conditions, and as such, it has neither birth nor death. "Without birth or death, eternal, ever-existing is this soul of man."[12]

वासांसि जीर्णानि यथा विहाय नवानि गृह्णाति नरोऽपराणि।
तथा शरीराणि विहाय जीर्णानि अन्यानि संयाति नवानि देही ॥२२॥

As the embodied person throws away a worn out dress and puts on a new one, so does the embodied Self discard worn out bodies and adopt other new ones. —2. 22

So far [we have discussed] God and nature, eternal God and eternal nature. What about souls? They also are eternal. No soul was [ever] created; neither can [the] soul die. Nobody can even imagine his own death. The soul is infinite, eternal. How can it die? It changes bodies. As a man takes off his old, worn-out garments and puts on new and fresh ones, even so the worn-out body is thrown away and [a] fresh body is taken.[13]

There are two sorts of races, the divine and the demonic. The divine think that they are soul and spirit. The demonic think that they are bodies. The old Indian philosophers tried to insist that the body is nothing. "As a man emits his old garment and takes a new one, even so the old body is [shed] and he takes a new one"[14]

नैनं छिन्दन्ति शस्त्राणि नैनं दहति पावकः ।
न चैनं क्लेदयन्त्यापो न शोषयति मारुतः ॥२३॥

No weapons can cut this Atman, no fire can burn It, no water can wet It, no air can dry It. —2. 23

अच्छेद्योऽयमदाह्योऽयमक्लेद्योऽशोष्य एव च ।
नित्यः सर्वगतः स्थाणुरचलोऽयं सनातनः ॥२४॥

This Self cannot be cut, nor can it be burnt, nor wetted, nor dried. Changeless, all-pervading, unmoving, immovable, this Self is eternal. —2. 24

We would describe the soul in these words: This soul the sword cannot cut, nor the spear pierce; the fire cannot burn nor water melt it; indestructible, omnipresent is this soul. Therefore weep not for it.[15]

So then the Hindu believes that he is a spirit. Him the sword cannot pierce—him the fire cannot burn—him the water cannot melt—him the air cannot dry. The Hindu believes that every soul is a circle whose circumference is nowhere, but whose centre is located in the body, and that death means the change of this centre from body to body. Nor is the soul bound by the conditions of matter. In its very essence it is free, unbounded, holy, pure, and perfect.[16]

Again, it follows that because the soul is not made of matter, since it is spiritual, it cannot obey the laws of matter, it cannot be judged by the laws of matter. It is, therefore, unconquerable, birthless, deathless, and changeless. "This Self, weapons cannot pierce, nor fire can burn, water cannot wet, nor air can dry up. Changeless, all-pervading, unmoving, immovable, eternal is this Self of man." We learn according to the Gita and the Vedanta that this individual Self is also *vibhu*, and according to Kapila, is omnipresent. Of course there are sects in India which hold that the Self is *anu*, infinitely small; but what they mean is *anu* in manifestation; its real nature is *vibhu*, all-pervading.[17]

You are all materialists, because you believe that you are the body. If a man gives me a hard punch, I would say I am punched. If he strikes me, I would say I am struck. If I am not the body, why should I say so? It makes no difference if I say I am the spirit. I am the body just now. I have converted myself into matter. That is why I am to renounce the body, to go back to what I really am. I am the spirit—the soul no instrument can pierce, no sword can cut asunder, no fire can burn, no air can dry. Unborn and uncreated, without beginning and without end, deathless, birthless and omnipresent—that is what I am; and all misery comes just because I think this little lump of clay is myself. I am identifying myself with matter and taking all the consequences.[18]

Let me tell you, strength, strength is what we want. And the first step in getting strength is to uphold the Upanishads, and believe—"I am the Soul", "Me the sword cannot cut; nor weapons pierce; me the fire cannot burn; me the air cannot dry; I am the Omnipotent, I am the Omniscient." So repeat these blessed, saving words. Do not say we are weak; we can do anything and everything. What can we not do? Everything can be done by us; we all have the same glorious soul, let us believe in it.[19]

The masses have been told all over the world that they are not human beings. They have been so frightened for centuries, till they have nearly become animals. Never were they allowed to hear of the Atman. Let them hear of the Atman—that even the lowest of the low have the Atman within, which never dies and never is born—of Him whom the sword cannot pierce, nor the fire burn, nor the air dry—immortal, without beginning or end, the all-pure, omnipotent, and omnipresent Atman! Let them have faith in themselves.[20]

The god went home, and at last found that he was the Self, beyond all thought, one without birth or death, whom the sword cannot pierce or the fire burn, whom the air cannot dry or the water melt, the beginningless and endless, the immovable, the intangible, the omniscient, the omnipotent Being; that It was neither the body nor the mind, but beyond them all. So he was satisfied; but the poor demon did not get the truth, owing to his fondness for the body.[21]

अव्यक्तादीनि भूतानि व्यक्तमध्यानि भारत ।
अव्यक्तनिधनान्येव तत्र का परिदेवना ॥२८॥

Beings come from the unseen, in between they become the seen, and they return also to the unseen; what is there to be worried about? —2. 28

Beings are unknown to our human senses before birth and after death. It is only in the interim that they are manifest. What is there to grieve about?[22]

आश्चर्यवत्पश्यति कश्चिदेनम् आश्चर्यवद्वदति तथैव चान्य: ।
आश्चर्यवच्चैनमन्य: शृणोति श्रुत्वाप्येनं वेद न चैव कश्चित् ॥२९॥

Some see this (truth) as a wonder; some others speak of It similarly as a wonder; some others hear about It as a wonder; some others even after hearing of It, do not understand it at all. —2. 29

Some look at It [the Self] with wonder. Some talk of It as wonderful. Others hear of It as wonderful. Others, hearing of It, do not understand.[23]

In the Ramakrishna Incarnation there is knowledge, devotion and love—infinite knowledge, infinite love, infinite work, infinite compassion for all beings. You have not yet been able to understand him. "श्रुत्वाप्येनं वेद न चैव कश्चित्—Even after hearing about Him, most people do not understand Him." What the whole Hindu race has thought in ages, he lived in one life. His life is the living commentary to the Vedas of all nations. People will come to know him by degrees.[24]

But it falleth out, that many who often hear the Gospel of Christ, are yet but little affected, because they are void of the Spirit of Christ. But whosoever would fully and feelingly understand the words of Christ, must endeavour to conform his life wholly to the life of Christ.[25] (*The Imitation of Christ*, V. 2.)*

स्वधर्ममपि चावेक्ष्य न विकम्पितुमर्हसि ।
धर्म्याद्धि युद्धाच्छ्रेयोऽन्यत्क्षत्रियस्य न विद्यते ॥३१॥

From the point of view of your own dharma, it is not fit for you to waver; for a *kshatriya* there is nothing more auspicious than a just war. —2. 31

But if you say that killing all these people is sinful, then consider this from the standpoint of your own caste-duty.[26]

---

*This passage is the English version of Swami Vivekananda's translation of *The Imitation of Christ* (V. 2) into Bengali. To this he had supplied the following footnote referring to the Gita (2. 29): श्रुत्वाप्येनं वेद न चैव कश्चित्। "Others, hearing of It, do not understand."

हतो वा प्राप्स्यसि स्वर्गं जित्वा वा भोक्ष्यसे महीम् ।
तस्मादुत्तिष्ठ कौन्तेय युद्धाय कृतनिश्चयः ।।३७।।

If you are killed, you will get heaven meant for heroes. Or, if you conquer, you will enjoy the earth; therefore, stand up, O Arjuna, with the firm determination to fight. —2. 37

Disciple: Where shall I get the capital for the business?

Swamiji: I shall somehow give you a start; for the rest you must depend on your own exertions. "If you die, you get to heaven; and if you win, you enjoy the earth." Even if you die in this attempt, well and good, many will take up the work, following your example. And if you succeed, you will live a life of great opulence.[27]

सुखदुःखे समे कृत्वा लाभालाभौ जयाजयौ ।
ततो युद्धाय युज्यस्व नैवं पापमवाप्स्यसि ।।३८।।

Having made pain and pleasure, gain and loss, conquest and defeat, the same, engage yourself then in battle. So shall you incur no sin. —2. 38

"Making pleasure and misery the same, making success and defeat the same, do thou stand up and fight."[28]

When I became a *sannyasin*, I consciously took the step, knowing that this body would have to die of starvation. What of that, I am a beggar. My friends are poor, I love the poor, I welcome poverty. I am glad that I sometimes have to starve. I ask help of none. What is the use? Truth will preach itself, it will not die for the want of the helping hands of me! "Making happiness and misery the same, making success and failure the same, fight thou on." It is that eternal love, unruffled equanimity under all circumstances, and perfect freedom from jealousy or animosity that will tell. That will tell, nothing else.[29]

एषा तेऽभिहिता सांख्ये बुद्धियोंगे त्विमां शृणु ।
बुद्ध्या युक्तो यया पार्थ कर्मबन्धं प्रहास्यसि ॥३९॥

The wisdom of Self-realization has been declared unto you.
Hear now the wisdom of yoga, endued with which, O son of
Pritha, you shall break through the bonds of karma. —2. 39

This is the beginning of another peculiar doctrine of the
Gita—the doctrine of non-attachment. That is to say, we have to
bear the result of our own actions because we attach ourselves to
them. "Only what is done as duty for duty's sake … can scatter
the bondage of karma."[30]

नेहाभिक्रमनाशोऽस्ति प्रत्यवायो न विद्यते ।
स्वल्पमप्यस्य धर्मस्य त्रायते महतो भयात् ॥४०॥

In this, there is no waste of unfinished attempt, nor is there
production of contrary results. Even a little of this dharma
protects (one) from great fear. —2. 40

There is no danger that you can overdo it. "If you do even a
little of it, [this yoga will save you from the terrible round of birth
and death]."[31]

We worship him* as God incarnate, the greatest, the boldest
preacher of morality that the world ever saw, the greatest *karma-
yogi*; as disciple of himself, as it were, the same Krishna came to
show how to make his† theories practical. There came once again
the same voice that in the Gita preached, "Even the least bit done
of this religion saves from great fear."[32]

This is teaching on the practical side. Believe, therefore, in
yourselves, and if you want material wealth, work it out; it will
come to you. If you want to be intellectual, work it out on the
intellectual plane, and intellectual giants you shall be. And if you

* Gautama Buddha.
† Krishna's.

want to attain to freedom, work it out on the spiritual plane, and free you shall be and shall enter into Nirvana, the Eternal Bliss. But one defect which lay in the Advaita was its being worked out so long on the spiritual plane only, and nowhere else; now the time has come when you have to make it practical. It shall no more be a *rahasya*, a secret, it shall no more live with monks in cave and forests, and in the Himalayas; it must come down to the daily, everyday life of the people; it shall be worked out in the palace of the king, in the cave of the recluse; it shall be worked out in the cottage of the poor, by the beggar in the street, everywhere; anywhere it can be worked out. Therefore do not fear whether you are a woman or a *shudra**, for this religion is so great, says Lord Krishna, that even a little of it brings a great amount of good.[33]

Cannot the knowledge, by which is attained even freedom from the bondage of worldly existence, bring ordinary material prosperity? Certainly it can. Freedom, dispassion, renunciation, all these are the very highest ideals, but "स्वल्पमप्यस्य धर्मस्य त्रायते महतो भयात्—Even a little of this dharma saves one from the great fear (of birth and death)." Dualist, qualified-monist, monist, Shaiva, Vaishnava, Shakta, even the Buddhist and the Jain and others— whatever sects have arisen in India—are all at one in this respect that infinite power is latent in this *jivatman* (individualized soul); from the ant to the perfect man there is the same Atman in all, the difference being only in manifestation. "As a farmer breaks the obstacles (to the course of water)" (Patanjali's *Yoga-Sutra*, Kaivalyapada, 3). That power manifests as soon as it gets the opportunity and the right place and time. From the highest god to the meanest grass, the same power is present in all—whether manifested or not. We shall have to call forth that power by going from door to door.[34]

---

* A person belonging to the lowest caste in the Hindu society.

A very small amount of religious work performed brings a large amount of result. If this statement of the Gita wanted an illustration, I am finding every day the truth of that great saying in my humble life.[35]

व्यवसायात्मिका बुद्धिरेकेह कुरुनन्दन ।
बहुशाखा ह्यनन्ताश्च बुद्धयोऽव्यवसायिनाम् ॥ ४१ ॥

In this, O scion of Kuru, there is but a single *buddhi* with a one-pointed determination. The purposes of the undecided are innumerable and many-branching. —2. 41

यामिमां पुष्पितां वाचं प्रवदन्त्यविपश्चितः ।
वेदवादरताः पार्थ नान्यदस्तीति वादिनः ॥ ४२ ॥

They are the unwise who utter flowery speeches, O Arjuna. They delight in the letter of the Vedas and argue that there is nothing else. —2. 42

कामात्मानः स्वर्गपरा जन्मकर्मफलप्रदाम् ।
क्रियाविशेषबहुलां भोगैश्वर्यगतिं प्रति ॥ ४३ ॥

They are full of desires, consider heaven as the highest which yield the fruit of rebirth and actions, and are full of specific rites that yield enjoyment and power. —2. 43

भोगैश्वर्यप्रसक्तानां तयापहृतचेतसाम् ।
व्यवसायात्मिका बुद्धिः समाधौ न विधीयते ॥ ४४ ॥

Those who have given themselves to pleasures and power, whose minds have been enslaved by them, there is no chance of developing that *buddhi* or determination which leads to *samadhi*. —2. 44

"Know, Arjuna, the mind that succeeds is the mind that is concentrated. The minds that are taken up with two thousand subjects (have) their energies dispersed. Some can talk flowery language and think there is nothing beyond the Vedas. They want to go to heaven. They want good things through the power of the Vedas, and so they make sacrifices." Such will never attain any success [in spiritual life] unless they give up all these materialistic ideas. That is another great lesson. Spirituality can never be attained unless all material ideas are given up. ... What is in the senses? The senses are all delusion. People wish to retain them [in heaven] even after they are dead—a pair of eyes, a nose. Some imagine they will have more organs than they have now. They want to see God sitting on a throne through all eternity—the material body of God. ... Such men's desires are for the body, for food and drink and enjoyment. It is the materialistic life prolonged. Man cannot think of anything beyond this life. This life is all for the body. "Such a man never comes to that concentration which leads to freedom."[36]

> त्रैगुण्यविषया वेदा निस्त्रैगुण्यो भवार्जुन ।
> निर्द्वन्द्वो नित्यसत्त्वस्थो नियोगक्षेम आत्मवान् ॥ ४५ ॥

The Vedas deal with the three *guna*s. Be you free, O Arjuna, from the triad of the *guna*s, free from the pairs of opposites, ever-balanced, free from the thought of getting and keeping, and established in the Self. —2. 45

"The Vedas only teach things belonging to the three *guna*s, to *sattva*, *rajas*, and *tamas*." The Vedas only teach about things in nature. People cannot think anything they do not see on earth. If they talk about heaven, they think of a king sitting on a throne, of people burning incense. It is all nature, nothing beyond nature. The Vedas, therefore, teach nothing but nature. "Go beyond nature, beyond the dualities of existence, beyond your own consciousness, caring for nothing, neither for good nor for evil."[37]

"Go thou beyond the scriptures, because they teach only up to nature, up to the three qualities." When we go beyond them, we find the harmony, and not before.[38]

The greatest name man ever gave to God is Truth. Truth is the fruit of realization; therefore seek it within the soul. Get away from all books and forms and let your soul see its Self. "We are deluded and maddened by books", Shri Krishna declares. Be beyond the dualities of nature. The moment you think creed and form and ceremony the "be-all" and "end-all", then you are in bondage. Take part in them to help others, but take care they do not become a bondage.[39]

कर्मण्येवाधिकारस्ते मा फलेषु कदाचन ।
मा कर्मफलहेतुर्भूः मा ते सङ्गोऽस्त्वकर्मणि ॥ ४७ ॥

Your right is to work only; but never to the fruits thereof. May you not be motivated by the fruits of actions; nor let your attachment be towards inaction. —2. 47

"To work we have the right, but not to the fruits thereof." Leave the fruits alone. Why care for results? If you wish to help a man, never think what that man's attitude should be towards you. If you want to do a great or a good work, do not trouble to think what the result will be.[40]

The *karma-yogi* asks why you require any motive to work other than the inborn love of freedom. Be beyond the common worldly motives. "To work you have the right, but not to the fruits thereof." Man can train himself to know and to practise that, says the *karma-yogi*. When the idea of doing good becomes a part of his very being, then he will not seek for any motive outside. Let us do good because it is good to do good; he who does good work even in order to get to heaven binds himself down, says the *karma-yogi*. Any work that is done with any the least selfish motive, instead of making us free, forges one more chain for our feet.[41]

Krishna did everything but without any attachment; he was in the world, but not of it. "Do all work but without attachment; work for work's sake, never for yourself."[42]

How hard it is to arrive at this sort of non-attachment! Therefore Krishna shows us the lower ways and methods. The easiest way for everyone is to do [his or her] work and not take the results. It is our desire that binds us. If we take the results of actions, whether good or evil, we will have to bear them. But if we work not for ourselves, but all for the glory of the Lord, the results will take care of themselves. "To work you have the right, but not to the fruits thereof." The soldier works for no results. He does his duty. If defeat comes, it belongs to the general, not to the soldier. We do our duty for love's sake—love for the general, love for the Lord.[43]

What is your motive? Are you sure that you are not actuated by greed of gold, by thirst for fame, or power? Are you really sure that you can stand to your ideals, and work on, even if the whole world wants to crush you down? Are you sure you know what you want and will perform your duty, and that alone, even if your life is at stake? Are you sure that you will persevere so long as life endures, so long as there is one pulsation left in the heart? Then you are a real reformer, you are a teacher, a Master, a blessing to mankind. But man is so impatient, so short-sighted! He has not the patience to wait, he has not the power to see. He wants to rule, he wants results immediately. Why? He wants to reap the fruits himself, and does not really care for others. Duty for duty's sake is not what he wants. "To work you have the right, but not to the fruits thereof," says Krishna. Why cling to results? Ours are the duties. Let the fruits take care of themselves. But man has no patience. He takes up any scheme. The larger number of would-be reformers all over the world, can be classed under this heading.[44]

"To be weak is to be miserable", says Milton. Doing and suffering are inseparably joined. (Often, too, the man who laughs most is the one who suffers most.) "To work you have the right, not to the fruits thereof."[45]

This world is not for cowards. Do not try to fly. Look not for success or failure. Join yourself to the perfectly unselfish will and work on. Know that the mind which is born to succeed joins itself to a determined will and perseveres. You have the right to work, but do not become so degenerate as to look for results. Work incessantly, but see something behind the work. Even good deeds can find a man in great bondage. Therefore be not bound by good deeds or by desire for name and fame. Those who know this secret pass beyond this round of birth and death and become immortal.[46]

Those great masterminds producing momentous results in the hearts of mankind were content to write their books without even putting their names, and to die quietly, leaving the books to posterity. Who knows the writers of our philosophy, who knows the writers of our Puranas? They all pass under the generic name of Vyasa, and Kapila, and so on. They have been true children of Shri Krishna. They have been true followers of the Gita; they practically carried out the great mandate, "To work you have the right, but not to the fruits thereof."[47]

By the by, I have made a discovery as to the mental method of really practising what the Gita teaches, of working without an eye to results. I have seen much light on concentration and attention and control of concentration, which if practised will take us out of all anxiety and worry. It is really the science of bottling up our minds whenever we like.[48]

Despair not; remember the Lord says in the Gita, "To work you have the right, but not to the result." Gird up your loins, my boy.[49]

Though the ideal of work of our *Brahmavadin* should always be "कर्मण्येवाधिकारस्ते मा फलेषु कदाचन—To work thou hast the right, but never to the fruits thereof", yet no sincere worker passes out of the field of activity without making himself known and catching at least a few rays of light.[50]

Bring all light into the world. Light, bring light! Let light come unto every one; the task will not be finished till every one has reached the Lord. Bring light to the poor; and bring more light to the rich, for they require it more than the poor. Bring light to the ignorant, and more light to the educated, for the vanities of the education of our time are tremendous! Thus bring light to all and leave the rest unto the Lord, for in the words of the same Lord, "To work you have the right and not to the fruits thereof." "Let not your work produce results for you, and at the same time may you never be without work."[51]

Let me remind you again, "Thou hast the right to work but not to the fruits thereof." Stand firm like a rock. Truth always triumphs. Let the children of Shri Ramakrishna be true to themselves and everything will be all right. We may not live to see the outcome, but as sure as we live, it will come sooner or later. What India wants is a new electric fire to stir up a fresh vigour in the national veins. This was ever, and always will be, slow work. Be content to work, and, above all, be true to yourself.[52]

This wonderful national machine has worked through ages, this wonderful river of national life is flowing before us. Who knows, and who dares to say, whether it is good and how it shall move? Thousands of circumstances are crowding round it, giving it a special impulse, making it dull at one time and quicker at another. Who dares command its motion? Ours is only to work, as the Gita says, without looking for results. Feed the national life with the fuel it wants, but the growth is its own; none can dictate its growth to it.[53]

बुद्धियुक्तो जहातीह उभे सुकृतदुष्कृते ।
तस्माद्योगाय युज्यस्व योगः कर्मसु कौशलम् ॥ ५० ॥

Endued with this evenness of *buddhi*, one frees oneself in this very life, alike from virtue and vice; devote yourself, therefore, to this yoga. Yoga is efficiency in action. —2. 50

Our karma determines what we deserve and what we can assimilate. We are responsible for what we are; and whatever we wish ourselves to be, we have the power to make ourselves. If what we are now has been the result of our own past actions, it certainly follows that whatever we wish to be in future can be produced by our present actions; so we have to know how to act. You will say, "What is the use of learning how to work? Everyone works in some way or other in this world." But there is such a thing as frittering away our energies. With regard to *karma-yoga*, the Gita says that it is doing work with cleverness and as a science; by knowing how to work, one can obtain the greatest results.[54]

कर्मजं बुद्धियुक्ता हि फलं त्यक्त्वा मनीषिणः ।
जन्मबन्धविनिर्मुक्ताः पदं गच्छन्त्यनामयम् ॥ ५१ ॥

The wise, possessed of this evenness of mind, abandoning the fruits of their actions, freed for ever from the fetters of births, go to that state which is beyond all evil. —2. 51

यदा ते मोहकलिलं बुद्धिर्व्यतितरिष्यति ।
तदा गन्तासि निर्वेदं श्रोतव्यस्य श्रुतस्य च ॥ ५२ ॥

When your intellect crosses beyond the taint of illusion, then shall you attain to indifference, regarding things heard and things yet to be heard. —2. 52

श्रुतिविप्रतिपन्ना ते यदा स्थास्यति निश्चला ।
समाधावचला बुद्धिस्तदा योगमवाप्स्यसि ॥ ५३ ॥

When your intellect, tossed about by the conflict of opinions, has become immovable and firmly established in the Self, then you will attain Self-realization. —2. 53

Who can work without any attachment? That is the real question. Such a man is the same whether his work succeeds or fails. His heart does not give one false beat even if his whole life-work is burnt to ashes in a moment. "This is the sage who always works for work's sake without caring for the results. Thus he goes beyond the pain of birth and death. Thus he becomes free." Then he sees that this attachment is all delusion. The Self can never be attached. ... Then he goes beyond all the scriptures and philosophies. If the mind is deluded and pulled into a whirlpool by books and scriptures, what is the good of all these scriptures? One says this, another says that. What book shall you take? Stand alone! See the glory of your own soul, and see that you will have to work. Then you will become a man of firm will.[55]

The only way to understand Him and the universe is to go beyond reason, beyond consciousness. "When thou goest beyond the heard and the hearing, the thought and the thinking, then alone wilt thou come to Truth."[56]

अर्जुन उवाच –
Arjuna said:

स्थितप्रज्ञस्य का भाषा समाधिस्थस्य केशव ।
स्थितधी: किं प्रभाषेत किमासीत व्रजेत किम् ॥ ५४॥

What, O Keshava, is the description of a person of steady wisdom, merged in *samadhi*? How does the person of steady wisdom speak, how sit, how walk? —2. 54

श्रीभगवानुवाच –
Shri Bhagavan said:

प्रजहाति यदा कामान्सर्वान्पार्थ मनोगतान् ।
आत्मन्येवात्मना तुष्ट: स्थितप्रज्ञस्तदोच्यते ॥ ५५॥

When one completely casts away, O Partha, all the desires of the mind, satisfied in the Self alone by the Self, then he or she is said to be one of steady wisdom. —2. 55

दु:खेष्वनुद्विग्नमनाः सुखेषु विगतस्पृहः ।
वीतरागभयक्रोधः स्थितधीर्मुनिरुच्यते ॥ ५६ ॥

One whose mind is not shaken by adversity, who does not
hanker after happiness, who has become free from blind
attachment, fear, and anger, is indeed the *muni* or sage of
steady wisdom. —2.56

Arjuna asks: "Who is a person of established will?" [Krishna
answers:] "The man who has given up all desires, who desires
nothing, not even this life, nor freedom, nor gods, nor work,
nor anything. When he has become perfectly satisfied, he has
no more cravings." He has seen the glory of the Self and has
found that the world, and the gods, and heaven are … within
his own Self. Then the gods become no gods; death becomes no
death; life becomes no life. Everything has changed. "A man is
said to be [illumined] if his will has become firm, if his mind is
not disturbed by misery, if he does not desire any happiness, if he
is free of all [attachment], of all fear, of all anger.[57]

यदा संहरते चायं कूर्मोऽङ्गानीव सर्वशः ।
इन्द्रियाणि इन्द्रियार्थेभ्यः तस्य प्रज्ञा प्रतिष्ठिता ॥ ५८ ॥

When also, like the tortoise drawing its limbs, one can
completely withdraw the senses from their sense objects, his
or her wisdom becomes steady. —2.58

"As the tortoise can draw in his legs, and if you strike him,
not one foot comes out, even so the sage can draw all his sense-
organs inside," and nothing can force them out. Nothing can
shake him, no temptation or anything. Let the universe tumble
about him, it does not make one single ripple in his mind.[58]

As the tortoise tucks its feet and head inside the shell, and
you may kill it and break it in pieces, and yet it will not come
out, even so the character of that man who has control over his
motives and organs is unchangeably established. He controls his

own inner forces, and nothing can draw them out against his will. By this continuous reflex of good thoughts, good impressions moving over the surface of the mind, the tendency for doing good becomes strong, and as the result we feel able to control the *indriya*s (the sense-organs, the nerve-centres).[59]

विषया विनिवर्तन्ते निराहारस्य देहिनः ।
रसवर्जं रसोऽप्यस्य परं दृष्ट्वा निवर्तते ॥ ५९ ॥

Sense objects fall away from the abstinent person, leaving the longing behind. But even that longing ceases when one realizes the supreme. —2. 59

Then comes a very important question. Sometimes people fast for days. ... When the worst man has fasted for twenty days, he becomes quite gentle. Fasting and torturing themselves have been practised by people all over the world. Krishna's idea is that this is all nonsense. He says that the senses will for the moment recede from the man who tortures himself, but will emerge again with twenty times more [power]. ... What should you do? The idea is to be natural—no asceticism. Go on, work, only mind that you are not attached. The will can never be fixed strongly in the man who has not learnt and practised the secret of non-attachment.[60]

यततो ह्यपि कौन्तेय पुरुषस्य विपश्चितः ।
इन्द्रियाणि प्रमाथीनि हरन्ति प्रसभं मनः ॥ ६० ॥

The turbulent senses, O son of Kunti, do violently snatch away the mind of even a wise man who is striving after perfection. —2. 60

There is then no peace in the heart of a carnal man, nor in him that is addicted to outward things, but in the spiritual and devout man.[61] (*The Imitation of Christ*, V.2.)*

ध्यायतो विषयान्पुंसः सङ्गस्तेषूपजायते ।
सङ्गात् संजायते कामः कामात्क्रोधोऽभिजायते ॥ ६ २ ॥

Thinking of sense objects, attachment to them is formed (in a human being); from attachment rises desire to possess; and from longing, anger emerges. —2. 62

क्रोधाद्भवति संमोहः संमोहात्स्मृतिविभ्रमः ।
स्मृतिभ्रंशात् बुद्धिनाशो बुद्धिनाशात्प्रणश्यति ॥ ६ ३ ॥

From anger comes delusion, and from delusion loss of memory. From loss of memory comes the ruin of discriminative power, and from the ruin of discrimination, the person perishes. —2. 63

The proud and covetous can never rest. The poor and humble in spirit live together in all peace.

The man that is not yet perfectly dead to himself, is quickly tempted and overcome in small and trifling things.[62] (*The Imitation of Christ*, V.1.)†

---

* This passage is the English version of Swami Vivekananda's translation of *The Imitation of Christ* (V. 2) into Bengali. To this he had supplied the following footnote referring to the Gita (2. 60): यततो ह्यपि कौन्तेय पुरुषस्य विपश्चितः ।

† This passage is the English version of Swami Vivekananda's translation of *The Imitation of Christ* (V. 2) into Bengali. To this he had supplied the following footnote referring to the Gita (2. 62-63): ध्यायतो विषयान्पुंसः सङ्गस्तेषूपजायते ।

इन्द्रियाणां हि चरतां यन्मनोऽनुविधीयते ।
तदस्य हरति प्रज्ञां वायुर्नावमिवाम्भसि ॥ ६७ ॥

For, the mind, which follows in the wake of the wandering
senses, carries away his or her discrimination, as a wind
(carries away from its course) a ship on the waters. —2. 67

Whensoever a man desireth anything inordinately, he beco-
meth presently disquieted in himself.[63] (*The Imitation of Christ*,
V.1.)*

या निशा सर्वभूतानां तस्यां जागर्ति संयमी ।
यस्यां जाग्रति भूतानि सा निशा पश्यतो मुनेः ॥ ६९ ॥

That which is night to all beings, in that the self-controlled
wakes. That in which all beings are awake, is night to the
Self-seeing *muni*. —2. 69

"Where it is dark night for the [sense-bound] world, the
self-controlled [man] is awake. It is daylight for him. ... And
where the world is awake, the sage sleeps." Where is the world
awake? In the senses. People want to eat and drink and have
children, and then they die a dog's death. ... They are always
awake for the senses. Even their religion is just for that. They
invent a God to help them, to give them more women, more
money, more children—never a God to help them become more
godlike! "Where the whole world is awake, the sage sleeps. But
where the ignorant are asleep, there the sage keeps awake"—in
the world of light where man looks upon himself not as a bird,
not as an animal, not as a body, but as infinite spirit, deathless,

---

* This passage is the English version of Swami Vivekananda's translation
of *The Imitation of Christ* (V. 1) into Bengali. To this he had supplied
the following footnote referring to the Gita (2. 67): For the mind
which follows in the wake of the wandering senses carries away his
discrimination as a wind (carries away from its course) a boat on the
waters.

immortal. There, where the ignorant are asleep, and do not have time, nor intellect, nor power to understand, there the sage is awake. That is daylight for him.[64]

"Where the world is awake, there the man of self-control is sleeping. Where the world sleeps, there he is waking." May even the dust of the world never touch you, for, after all the poets may say, it is only a piece of carrion covered over with garlands. Touch it not—if you can.[65]

The end and aim of yoga is to realize God. To do this we must go beyond relative knowledge, go beyond the sense-world. The world is awake to the senses, the children of the Lord are asleep on that plane. The world is asleep to the Eternal, the children of the Lord are awake in that realm. These are the sons of God. There is but one way to control the senses—to see Him who is the Reality in the universe. Then and only then can we really conquer our senses.[66]

आपूर्यमाणमचलप्रतिष्ठं
　　समुद्रमापः प्रविशन्ति यद्वत् ।
तद्वत्कामा यं प्रविशन्ति सर्वे
　　स शान्तिमाप्नोति न कामकामी ॥ ७० ॥

As into the ocean, brimful and still, flow the (flood) waters (of various rivers without agitating the ocean), even so is the *muni* into whom enter all desires; he or she attains to peace, and not the desirer of desires. —2. 70

"As all the rivers of the world constantly pour their waters into the ocean, but the ocean's grand, majestic nature remains undisturbed and unchanged, so even though all the senses bring in sensations from nature, the ocean-like heart of the sage knows no disturbance, knows no fear." Let miseries come in millions of rivers and happiness in hundreds! I am no slave to misery! I am no slave to happiness![67]

CHAPTER III

अर्जुन उवाच –

Arjuna said:

ज्यायसी चेत् कर्मणस्ते मता बुद्धि: जनार्दन ।
तत् किं कर्मणि घोरे मां नियोजयसि केशव ॥ १ ॥

If, O Janardana (Krishna), according to you knowledge is superior to action, why then, O Keshava, do You engage me in this terrible action? —3. 1

व्यामिश्रेणेव वाक्येन बुद्धिं मोहयसीव मे ।
तदेकं वद निश्चित्य येन श्रेयोऽहमाप्नुयाम् ॥२॥

With these seemingly conflicting words, You are, as it were, bewildering my understanding; tell me that one thing for certain, by which I can attain to the Highest. —3. 2

श्रीभगवान् उवाच –

The Blessed Lord said:

लोकेऽस्मिन् द्विविधा निष्ठा पुरा प्रोक्ता मयानघ ।
ज्ञानयोगेन सांख्यानां कर्मयोगेन योगिनाम् ॥ ३ ॥

In the beginning (of creation), O sinless one, the twofold path was given by Me to this world—the path of knowledge for the Sankhyas, and the path of work for the Yogis. —3. 3

Arjuna asks: "You just advised action, and yet you uphold knowledge of Brahman as the highest form of life. Krishna, if you think that knowledge is better than action, why do you tell me to act?" [Shri Krishna]: "From ancient times these two systems have

60

come down to us. The Sankhya philosophers advance the theory of knowledge. The Yogis advance the theory of work.[1]

But it is a most difficult thing to give up the clinging to this universe; few ever attain to that. There are two ways to do that mentioned in our books. One is called the *"neti, neti"* (not this, not this), the other is called *"iti"* (this); the former is the negative, and the latter is the positive way. The negative way is the most difficult. It is only possible to the men of the very highest, exceptional minds and gigantic wills who simply stand up and say, "No, I will not have this," and the mind and body obey their will, and they come out successful. But such people are very rare. The vast majority of mankind choose the positive way, the way through the world, making use of all the bondages themselves to break those very bondages. This is also a kind of giving up; only it is done slowly and gradually, by knowing things, enjoying things and thus obtaining experience, and knowing the nature of things until the mind lets them all go at last and becomes unattached. The former way of obtaining non-attachment is by reasoning, and the latter way is through work and experience. The first is the path of *jnana-yoga* and is characterized by the refusal to do any work; the second is that of *karma-yoga*, in which there is no cessation from work.[2]

न कर्मणामनारम्भात् नैष्कर्म्यं पुरुषोऽश्नुते ।
न च संन्यसनादेव सिद्धिं समधिगच्छति ॥ ४ ॥

By non-performance of action, none reaches inaction; by merely giving up action, no one attains perfection. —3. 4

Krishna strikes another note as a teacher of intense activity. Work, work, work day and night, says the Gita. You may ask, "Then, where is peace? If all through life I am to work like a cart-horse and die in harness, what am I here for?" Krishna says, "Yes, you will find peace. Flying from work is never the way to find peace." Throw off your duties if you can, and go to the top of a mountain; even there the mind is going—whirling, whirling, whirling. Someone asked a *sannyasin*, "Sir, have you found a nice place? How many years have you been travelling in the Himalayas?" "For forty years," replied the *sannyasin*. "There are so many beautiful spots to select from, and to settle down in: why did you not do so?" "Because for these forty years my mind would not allow me to do so." We all say, "Let us find peace"; but the mind will not allow us to do so.[3]

न हि कश्चित्क्षणमपि जातु तिष्ठत्यकर्मकृत् ।
कार्यते ह्यवशः कर्म सर्वः प्रकृतिजैर्गुणैः ॥ ५ ॥

Verily, none can ever rest for even an instant, without performing action; for all are made to act, helplessly indeed, by the *guna*s (or forces) born of *prakriti* (nature). —3. 5

कर्मेन्द्रियाणि संयम्य य आस्ते मनसा स्मरन् ।
इन्द्रियार्थान् विमूढात्मा मिथ्याचारः स उच्यते ॥ ६ ॥

One who, restraining the organs of actions, sits revolving in the mind thoughts regarding sense objects, he or she, of deluded understanding, is called a hypocrite. —3. 6

यस्त्विन्द्रियाणि मनसा नियम्यारभतेऽर्जुन ।
कर्मेन्द्रियैः कर्मयोगमसक्तः स विशिष्यते ॥ ७ ॥

But, O Arjuna, one who, controlling the senses by the mind, and remaining unattached, directs the organs of action to the yoga of action, excels. —3. 7

But none can attain to peace by renouncing actions. None in this life can stop activity even for a moment. Nature's qualities [*guna*s] will make him act. He who stops his activities and at the same time is still thinking about them attains to nothing; he only becomes a hypocrite. But he who by the power of his mind gradually brings his sense-organs under control, employing them in work, that man is better. Therefore do thou work."[4]

यस्तु आत्मरतिरेव स्यात् आत्मतृप्तश्च मानव: ।
आत्मन्येव च सन्तुष्ट: तस्य कार्यं न विद्यते ॥ १७॥

But the person who is delighted in the Atman, satisfied in the Atman, and finds joy in the Atman alone, he or she has no obligatory duty to perform. —3. 17

"He whose joy is only in himself, whose desires are only in himself, he has learned his lessons." This is the great lesson that we are here to learn through myriads of births and heavens and hells—that there is nothing to be asked for, desired for, beyond one's Self.[5]

As the Gita says, "He whose devotion is to the Atman, he who does not want anything beyond Atman, he who has become satisfied in the Atman, what work is there for him to do?"[6]

The highest men are calm, silent, and unknown. They are the men who really know the power of thought; they are sure that even if they go into a cave and close the door and simply think five true thoughts and then pass away, these five thoughts of theirs will live through eternity. Indeed such thoughts will penetrate through the mountains, cross the oceans, and travel through the world. They will enter deep into human hearts and brains and raise up men and women who will give them practical expression in the workings of human life. These *sattvika* men are too near the Lord to be active and to fight, to be working, struggling, preaching, and doing good, as they say, here on earth to humanity. The active workers, however good, have still a little remnant of ignorance left in them. When our nature has yet some impurities left in it, then alone can we work. It is in the nature of work to be impelled ordinarily by motive and by attachment. In the presence of an ever active Providence who notes even the sparrow's fall, how can man attach any importance to his own work? Will it not be a blasphemy to do so when we know that He is taking care of the minutest things in the world? We have only to stand in awe and reverence before Him saying, "Thy will be done". The highest men cannot work, for in them there is no attachment. Those whose whole soul is gone into the Self, those whose desires are confined in the Self, who have become ever associated with the Self, for them there is no work. Such are indeed the highest of mankind; but apart from them every one else has to work.[7]

Every one must work in the universe. Only those who are perfectly satisfied with the Self, whose desires do not go beyond the Self, whose mind never strays out of the Self, to whom the Self is all in all, only those do not work. The rest must work.[8]

तस्मात् असक्त: सततं कार्यं कर्म समाचर ।
असक्तो ह्याचरन् कर्म परमाप्नोति पूरुष: ॥ १९ ॥

Therefore, do thou always perform obligatory actions, without attachment; by performing action without attachment, the human being attains to the highest. —3. 19

To work without motive, to work unattached, brings the highest bliss and freedom. This secret of *karma-yoga* is taught by the Lord Shri Krishna in the Gita.[9]

Disciple: But, sir, if one has to renounce the fruits of work, why should one be induced to undertake work which is always troublesome?

Swamiji: In this human life, one cannot help doing some kind of work always. When man has perforce to do some work, *karma-yoga* enjoins on him to do it in such a way as will bring freedom through the realization of the Atman.[10]

We also read this in the Gita and learn that we have to work, constantly work with all our power; to put our whole mind in the work, whatever it be, that we are doing. At the same time, we must not be attached. That is to say, we must not be drawn away from work by anything else; still, we must be able to quit the work whenever we like.[11]

That is the one cause of misery: we are attached, we are being caught. Therefore says the Gita: Work constantly; work, but be not attached; be not caught. Reserve unto yourself the power of detaching yourself from everything, however beloved, however much the soul might yearn for it, however great the pangs of misery you feel if you were going to leave it; still, reserve the power of leaving it whenever you want.[12]

कर्मणैव हि संसिद्धिमास्थिता जनकादयः ।
लोकसंग्रहमेवापि संपश्यन् कर्तुमर्हसि ॥ २० ॥

Verily, through action alone, Janaka and others attained perfection; even with the view to ensure *lokasamgraha*, the stability of human society, you should perform action. —3.20

यद्यद् आचरति श्रेष्ठः तत्तदेवेतरो जनः ।
स यत् प्रमाणं कुरुते लोकस्तत् अनुवर्तते ॥ २१ ॥

Whatever the superior person does, that is also followed by others; what standard he or she demonstrates by action, people follow that. —3.21

"Even if you have known the secret that you have no duty, that you are free, still you have to work for the good of others. Because whatever a great man does, ordinary people will do also."[13]

न मे पार्थास्ति कर्तव्यं त्रिषु लोकेषु किंचन ।
नानवाप्तमवाप्तव्यं वर्त एव च कर्मणि ॥ २२ ॥

I have, O Partha, no duty, nothing that I have not gained, and nothing that I have yet to gain, in the three worlds; yet, I do continue in action. —3.22

यदि ह्यहं न वर्तेयं जातु कर्मण्यतन्द्रितः ।
मम वर्त्मानुवर्तन्ते मनुष्याः पार्थ सर्वशः ॥ २३ ॥

If ever I did not continue to work without any relaxation, O Partha, men and women would, in every way follow my example. —3.23

उत्सीदेयुरिमे लोका न कुर्यां कर्म चेदहम् ।
सङ्करस्य च कर्ता स्यामुपहन्यामिमाः प्रजाः ॥२४॥

If I did not do work, these worlds would perish, I would be the cause of social disruption and I would also be ruining these people. —3. 24

[The following paragraph is a reference to verse 22.]

Our best work is done, our greatest influence is exerted, when we are without thought of self. All great geniuses know this. Let us open ourselves to the one Divine Actor, and let Him act, and do nothing ourselves. "O Arjuna! I have no duty in the whole world", says Krishna. Be perfectly resigned, perfectly unconcerned; then alone can you do any true work. No eyes can see the real forces, we can only see the results. Put out self, lose it, forget it; just let God work, it is His business. We have nothing to do but stand aside and let God work. The more we go away, the more God comes in. Get rid of the little "I", and let only the great "I" live.[14]

[The following paragraphs refer to verses 22 to 24.]

Work day and night! "Behold, I am the Lord of the Universe. I have no duty. Every duty is bondage. But I work for work's sake. If I ceased to work for a minute, [there would be chaos]." So do thou work, without any idea of duty.[15]

Krishna says, "Look at Me, Arjuna! If I stop from work for one moment, the whole universe will die. I have nothing to gain from work; I am the one Lord, but why do I work? Because I love the world." God is unattached because He loves; that real love makes us unattached.[16]

If a great man who has attained peace of mind and freedom ceases to work, then all the rest without that knowledge and peace will try to imitate him, and thus confusion would arise. "Behold, Arjuna, there is nothing that I do not possess and nothing that I want to acquire. And yet I continue to work. If I stopped work for a moment, the whole universe would [be destroyed]."[17]

[The following paragraph is a reference to verses 23 & 24.]

The first is the question of creation, that this nature, Prakriti, Maya is infinite, without beginning. It is not that this world was created the other day, not that a God came and created the world and since that time has been sleeping; for that cannot be. The creative energy is still going on. God is eternally creating—is never at rest. Remember the passage in the Gita where Krishna says, "If I remain at rest for one moment, this universe will be destroyed." If that creative energy which is working all around us, day and night, stops for a second, the whole thing falls to the ground. There never was a time when that energy did not work throughout the universe, but there is the law of cycles, *pralaya*.[18]

[The following paragraph is a reference to verse 24.]

Thus the vital point of our national life has been touched; otherwise, why should we sink to this degraded state? Read in the Gita, "सङ्करस्य च कर्ता स्यामुपहन्यामिमाः प्रजाः—I should then be the cause of the admixture of races, and I should thus ruin these beings." How came this terrible *varna-samkarya*—this confounding mixture of all castes—and disappearance of all qualitative distinctions? Why has the white complexion of our forefathers now become black? Why did the *sattva-guna* give place to the prevailing *tamas* with a sprinkling, as it were, of *rajas* in it? That is a long story to tell, and I reserve my answer for some future occasion. For the present, try to understand this, that if the *jati dharma** be rightly and truly preserved, the nation shall never fall.[19]

---

* *Jati dharma*, that is, the dharma enjoined according to the different castes—the *svadharma*, that is, one's own dharma, or set of duties prescribed for man according to his capacity and position—which is the very basis of Vedic religion and Vedic society.[21]

सक्ता: कर्मण्यविद्वांसो यथा कुर्वन्ति भारत ।
कुर्यात् विद्वान् तथा असक्त: चिकीर्षु: लोकसंग्रहम् ॥ २५ ॥

As the unenlightened, attached to work, acts, so should the
enlightened act, O descendent of Bharata, but without attachment, desirous of the well-being of the world. —3. 25

"That which the ignorant do with desire for results and gain,
let the wise do without any attachment and without any desire
for results and gain."20

न बुद्धिभेदं जनयेत् अज्ञानां कर्मसङ्गिनाम् ।
जोषयेत् सर्वकर्माणि विद्वान् युक्त: समाचरन् ॥ २६ ॥

One should not unsettle the understanding of the ignorant,
who are attached to action; the enlightened one, oneself
steadily acting in the yoga spirit, should engage the ignorant
also in all work. —3. 26

Q.—Are sects, ceremonies, and scriptures helps to
realization?

A.—When a man realizes, he gives up everything. The various
sects and ceremonies and books, so far as they are the means of
arriving at that point, are all right. But when they fail in that,
we must change them. "The knowing one must not despise the
condition of those who are ignorant, nor should the knowing one
destroy the faith of the ignorant in their own particular method,
but by proper action lead them and show them the path to come
to where he stands."22

Speak out the truth boldly, without any fear that it will puzzle
the weak. Men are selfish; they do not want others to come up
to the same level of their knowledge, for fear of losing their own
privilege and prestige over others. Their contention is that the
knowledge of the highest spiritual truths will bring about confusion
in the understanding of the weak-minded men, and so the *shloka*
goes: "One should not unsettle the understanding of the ignorant,

attached to action (by teaching them *jnana*): the wise man, himself steadily acting, should engage the ignorant in all work."[23]

What right have you to say that this man's method is wrong? It may be wrong for you. That is to say, if you undertake the method, you will be degraded; but that does not mean that he will be degraded. Therefore, says Krishna, if you have knowledge and see a man weak, do not condemn him. Go to his level and help him if you can. He must grow.[24]

Even if you have knowledge, do not disturb the childlike faith of the ignorant. On the other hand, go down to their level and gradually bring them up. That is a very powerful idea, and it has become the ideal in India. That is why you can see a great philosopher going into a temple and worshipping images. It is not hypocrisy.[25]

प्रकृतेः क्रियमाणानि गुणैः कर्माणि सर्वशः ।
अहङ्कारविमूढात्मा कर्ताहमिति मन्यते ॥२७॥

The *gunas* of *prakriti* perform all actions; with the understanding deluded by egotism, the human being thinks, "I am the doer." —3. 27

"Therefore, Arjuna, all these actions are in nature. Nature ... is working out her own laws in our bodies and minds. We identify ourselves with nature and say, 'I am doing this.' This way delusion seizes us." We always act under some compulsion. When hunger compels me, I eat. And suffering is still worse—slavery. That real "I" is eternally free. What can compel it to do anything? The sufferer is in nature. It is only when we identify ourselves with the body that we say, "I am suffering; I am Mr. So-and-so"—all such nonsense. But he who has known the truth, holds himself aloof. Whatever his body does, whatever his mind does, he does not care. But mind you, the vast majority of mankind are under this delusion; and whenever they do any good, they feel that they are [the doers].[26]

मयि सर्वाणि कर्माणि संन्यस्याध्यात्मचेतसा ।
निराशी: निर्ममो भूत्वा युध्यस्व विगतज्वर: ॥ ३ ० ॥

Renouncing all actions to Me, with mind centred on the
Self, getting rid of hope and selfishness, fight on, free from
mental fever. —3. 30

"Surrendering the fruits of work to God" is to take to ourselves neither credit nor blame, but to give up both to the Lord
and be at peace.[27]

The Gita teaches that all works should be done thus. He
who is one with the Lord through yoga performs all his works
by becoming immersed in concentration, and does not seek any
personal benefit. Such a performance of work brings only good to
the world, no evil can come out of it. Those who work thus never
do anything for themselves.[28]

सदृशं चेष्टते स्वस्या: प्रकृते: ज्ञानवानपि ।
प्रकृतिं यान्ति भूतानि निग्रह: किं करिष्यति ॥ ३ ३ ॥

Even a wise person acts in accordance with his or her own
nature; beings follow nature; what can suppression do? —3. 33

"Even those who know the path act impelled by their
own nature. Everyone acts according to his nature. He cannot
transcend it." The atom cannot disobey the law. Whether it is the
mental or the physical atom, it must obey the law. "What is the
use of [external restraint]?"[29]

"Nature will have her way. What can suppression do?" That is
a terrible [statement] in the Gita. It seems it may be a vain struggle
after all. You may have a hundred thousand [urges competing]
at the same time. You may repress [them], but the moment the
spring rebounds, the whole thing is there again.[30]

श्रेयान् स्वधर्मो विगुणः परधर्मात् स्वनुष्ठितात् ।
स्वधर्मे निधनं श्रेयः परधर्मो भयावहः ॥ ३५ ॥

Better is one's own dharma, though imperfect, than the
dharma of another well performed; better is death in one's
own dharma; another person's dharma is fraught with fear.
—3. 35

Shri Krishna says: "Better die in your own path than attempt
the path of another." This is my path, and I am down here. And
you are way up there, and I am always tempted to give up my path
thinking I will go there and be with you. And if I go up, I am
neither there nor here. We must not lose sight of this doctrine.
It is all [a matter of] growth. Wait and grow, and you attain
everything; otherwise there will be [great spiritual danger]. Here
is the fundamental secret of teaching religion.[31]

Therefore, better die working out your own natural religion
than following another's natural religion, however great it may
appear to you.[32]

Every man should take up his own ideal and endeavour to
accomplish it. That is a surer way of progress than taking up other
men's ideals, which he can never hope to accomplish. For instance,
we take a child and at once give him the task of walking twenty
miles. Either the little one dies, or one in a thousand crawls the
twenty miles, to reach the end exhausted and half-dead. That is
like what we generally try to do with the world. All the men and
women, in any society, are not of the same mind, capacity, or of
the same power to do things; they must have different ideals, and
we have no right to sneer at any ideal. Let every one do the best
he can for realizing his own ideal. Nor is it right that I should be
judged by your standard or you by mine. The apple tree should
not be judged by the standard of the oak, nor the oak by that
of the apple. To judge the apple tree you must take the apple
standard, and for the oak, its own standard.[33]

काम एष क्रोध एष रजोगुण समुद्भवः ।
महाशनो महापाप्मा विद्ध्येनमिह वैरिणम् ॥ ३७ ॥

It is sensual desire, it is anger, born of the *rajo-guna*; of great craving and of great sin; know this as the enemy here (in human life). —3. 37

आवृतं ज्ञानमेतेन ज्ञानिनो नित्यवैरिणा ।
कामरूपेण कौन्तेय दुष्पूरेण अनलेन च ॥ ३९ ॥

Knowledge is covered by this, the constant foe of the wise, O son of Kunti, the unappeasable fire in the form of (unrestrained sensual) desire. —3. 39

इन्द्रियाणि मनो बुद्धिः अस्याधिष्ठानमुच्यते ।
एतैः विमोहयत्येष ज्ञानमावृत्य देहिनम् ॥ ४० ॥

The sense organs, the mind and the intellect are said to be its abodes; through these it deludes the embodied soul by veiling its wisdom. —3. 40

Beware, Arjuna, lust and anger are the great enemies. These are to be controlled. These cover the knowledge even of those [who are wise]. This fire of lust is unquenchable. Its location is in the sense-organs and in the mind. The Self desires nothing.[34]

CHAPTER IV

श्रीभगवान् उवाच –

Shri Krishna said:

इमं विवस्वते योगं प्रोक्तवान् अहमव्ययम् ।
विवस्वान् मनवे प्राह मनुरिक्ष्वाकवेऽब्रवीत् ॥ १ ॥

I told this imperishable yoga to Vivasvan; Vivasvan told it to Manu; (and) Manu told it to Ikshvaku: —4. 1

एवं परम्पराप्राप्तमिमं राजर्षयो विदुः ।
स कालेनेह महता योगो नष्टः परन्तप ॥ २ ॥

Thus handed down in regular succession, the royal sages knew this yoga; this yoga, by long lapse of time, declined in this world, O scorcher of foes. —4. 2

स एवांयं मया तेऽद्य योगः प्रोक्तः पुरातनः ।
भक्तोऽसि मे सखा चेति रहस्यं ह्येतद् उत्तमम् ॥ ३ ॥

I have this day told you that same supremely profound ancient yoga considering you as my devotee and my friend. —4. 3

अर्जुन उवाच –

Arjuna said:

अपरं भवतो जन्म परं जन्म विवस्वतः ।
कथमेतद् विजानीयां त्वमादौ प्रोक्तवान् इति ॥ ४ ॥

Later was your birth, and that of Vivasvat prior; how then should I understand that you spoke about this earlier? —4. 4

"This yoga I taught in ancient times [to Vivasvan; Vivasvan taught it to Manu]. ... Thus it was that the knowledge descended from one thing to another. But in time this great yoga was destroyed. That is why I am telling it to you again today." Then Arjuna asks, "Why do you speak thus? You are a man born only the other day, and [Vivasvan was born long before you]. What do you mean that you taught him?"[1]

श्रीभगवान् उवाच —
The Blessed Lord said:

बहूनि मे व्यतीतानि जन्मानि तव चार्जुन ।
तान्यहं वेद सर्वाणि न त्वं वेत्थ परन्तप ॥ ५ ॥

Many are the births that have been passed through by me and by you, O Arjuna; I know them all, while you do not know, O scorcher of foes. —4. 5*

अजोऽपि सन् अव्ययात्मा भूतानामीश्वरोऽपि सन् ।
प्रकृतिं स्वामधिष्ठाय सम्भवाम्यात्ममायया ॥ ६ ॥

Though I am unborn, of changeless nature, and Lord of all beings, yet subjugating my *prakriti* or divine nature, I am born by my own *maya*. —4. 6

"Both you and I have passed through many births; you know them not, I know them all."[2]

Then Krishna says, "O Arjuna, you and I have run the cycle of births and deaths many times, but you are not conscious of them all. I am without beginning, birthless, the absolute Lord of all creation. I through my own nature take form ... ."[3]

---

* With this verse Swamiji opened his piece of writing on "Reincarnation", contributed to the *Metaphysical Magazine*, New York (March 1895).

यदा यदा हि धर्मस्य ग्लानिर्भवति भारत ।
अभ्युत्थानमधर्मस्य तदात्मानं सृजाम्यहम् ॥ ७ ॥

Whenever, O descendant of Bharata, there is decline of
dharma, and rise of adharma, then I body myself forth. —4. 7

परित्राणाय साधूनां विनाशाय च दुष्कृताम् ।
धर्मसंस्थापनार्थाय संभवामि युगे युगे ॥ ८ ॥

For the protection of the virtuous, for the destruction of the
wicked, and for the establishment of dharma, I come into
being in every age. —4. 8

[The following paragraph is a reference to verses 6 to 8, and
the rest refer to 7 and 8.]

In India they have the same idea of the Incarnations of God.
One of their great Incarnations, Krishna, whose grand sermon,
the *Bhagavad Gita*, some of you might have read, says, "Though
I am unborn, of changeless nature, and Lord of beings, yet
subjugating My Prakriti, I come into being by My own Maya.
Whenever virtue subsides and immorality prevails, then I body
Myself forth. For the protection of the good, for the destruction
of the wicked, and for the establishment of dharma, I come into
being, in every age." Whenever the world goes down, the Lord
comes to help it forward; and so He does from time to time and
place to place.[4]

A Hindu philosopher would say: These are the great souls;
they are already free. And though free, they refuse to accept their
liberation while the whole world is suffering. They come again
and again, take a human embodiment and help mankind. They
know from their childhood what they are and what they come for.
... They do not come through bondage like we do. ... They come
out of their own free will, and cannot help having tremendous
spiritual power. We cannot resist it. The vast mass of mankind is
dragged into the whirlpool of spirituality, and the vibration goes
on and on because one of these [great souls] gives a push. So it

continues until all mankind is liberated and the play of this planet is finished.[5]

Whenever virtue subsides and wickedness prevails, I come to help mankind. For the salvation of the good, for the destruction of wickedness, for the establishment of spirituality I come from time to time.[6]

"Whenever virtue subsides and immorality abounds, I take human form. In every age I come for the salvation of the good, for the destruction of the wicked, for the establishment of spirituality."[7]

God understands human failings and becomes man to do good to humanity: "Whenever virtue subsides and wickedness prevails, I manifest Myself. To establish virtue, to destroy evil, to save the good I come from *yuga* (age) to *yuga*."[8]

God understands human failings and becomes a man to do good to humanity. "Whenever virtue subsides and immorality prevails, then I come to help mankind", says Krishna.[9]

"Whenever virtue subsides and vice prevails, I come down to help mankind," declares Krishna, in the *Bhagavad Gita*. Whenever this world of ours, on account of growth, on account of added circumstances, requires a new adjustment, a wave of power comes; and as man is acting on two planes, the spiritual and the material, waves of adjustment come on both planes.[10]

"Whenever virtue subsides, and wickedness raises its head, I manifest Myself to restore the glory of religion"—are the words, O noble Prince,* of the Eternal One in the holy Gita, striking the keynote of the pulsating ebb and flow of the spiritual energy in the universe. These changes are manifesting themselves again and again in rhythms peculiar to themselves, and like every other tremendous change, though affecting, more or less, every particle within their sphere of action, they show their effects more

---

* The Raja of Khetri.

intensely upon those particles which are naturally susceptible to their power.[11]

Religious knowledge became complete when *Tat Twam Asi* (Thou art That) was discovered, and that was in the Vedas. What remained was the guidance of people from time to time according to different times and places, according to different circumstances and environments; people had to be guided along the old, old path, and for this these great teachers came, these great sages. Nothing can bear out more clearly this position than the celebrated saying of Shri Krishna in the Gita: "Whenever virtue subsides and irreligion prevails, I create Myself for the protection of the good; for the destruction of all immorality I am coming from time to time." This is the idea in India.[12]

Our prophet says that whenever evil and immortality prevail on earth, He will come down and support His children; and this He is doing from time to time and from place to place. And whenever on earth you see an extraordinary holy man trying to uplift humanity, know that He is in him.[13]

Since the dawn of history, no missionary went out of India to propagate the Hindu doctrines and dogmas; but now a wonderful change is coming over us. Shri Bhagavan Krishna says, "Whenever virtue subsides and immorality prevails, then I come again and again to help the world." Religious researches disclose to us the fact that there is not a country possessing a good ethical code but has borrowed something of it from us, and there is not one religion possessing good ideas of the immortality of the soul but has derived it directly or indirectly from us.[14]

We read in the history of the world about prophets and their lives, and these come down to us through centuries of writings and workings by their disciples. Through thousands of years of chiselling and modelling, the lives of the great prophets of yore come down to us; and yet, in my opinion, not one stands so high in brilliance as that life which I saw with my own eyes, under whose shadow I have lived, at whose feet I have learnt everything—the life of Ramakrishna Paramahamsa. Ay, friends, you all know the celebrated saying of the Gita: "Whenever, O descendant of Bharata, there is decline of dharma, and rise of *adharma*, then I body Myself forth. For the protection of the good, for the destruction of the wicked, and for the establishment of dharma I come into being in every age."[15]

There are a great many similarities in the teaching of the *New Testament* and the Gita. The human thought goes the same way. ... I will find you the answer in the words of Krishna himself: "Whenever virtue subsides and irreligion prevails, I come down. Again and again I come. Therefore, whenever thou seest a great soul struggling to uplift mankind, know that I am come, and worship."[16]

The central figure of the Gita is Krishna. As you worship Jesus of Nazareth as God come down as man, so the Hindus worship many Incarnations of God. They believe in not one or two only, but in many, who have come down from time to time, according to the needs of the world, for the preservation of dharma and destruction of wickedness. Each sect has one, and Krishna is one of them.[17]

Life is short, but the soul is immortal and eternal, and one thing being certain, death, let us therefore take up a great ideal and give up our whole life to it. Let this be our determination, and may He, the Lord, who "comes again and again for the salvation of His own people", to quote from our scriptures—may the great Krishna bless us and lead us all to the fulfilment of our aims![18]

ये यथा मां प्रपद्यन्ते तांस्तथैव भजाम्यहम् ।
मम वर्त्मानुवर्तन्ते मनुष्याः पार्थ सर्वशः ॥ ११ ॥

In whatever way men and women worship me, in the same. way do I fulfil their desires; (it is) my path, O son of Pritha, (that) people tread, in all ways. —4. 11

The present convention, which is one of the most august assemblies ever held, is in itself a vindication, a declaration to the world of the wonderful doctrine preached in the Gita: "Whosoever comes to Me, through whatsoever form, I reach him; all men are struggling through paths which in the end lead to me." Sectarianism, bigotry, and its horrible descendant, fanaticism, have long possessed this beautiful earth. They have filled the earth with violence, drenched it often and often with human blood, destroyed civilization and sent whole nations to despair. Had it not been for these horrible demons, human society would be far more advanced than it is now. But their time is come; and I fervently hope that the bell that tolled this morning in honour of this convention may be the death-knell of all fanaticism, of all persecutions with the sword or with the pen, and of all uncharitable feelings between persons wending their way to the same goal.[19]

"Whosoever wants to reach me through whatsoever ways, I reach him through that. But know, Arjuna, none can ever swerve from my path." None ever did. How can we? None swerves from His path.[20]

Her* mother's heart could only be satisfied by conceiving God as her baby. Many and many a time her learned husband had talked to her of Him who is preached in the Vedas, the formless, the infinite, the impersonal. She listened with all attention, and the conclusion was always the same—what is written in the Vedas must be true; but, oh! it was so immense, so far off, and she, only a weak, ignorant woman; and then, it was also written: "In whatsoever form one seeks Me, I reach him in that form, for all mankind are but following the paths I laid down for them"—and that was enough. She wanted to know no more. And there she was—all of the devotion, of faith, of love her heart was capable

---

* The Gopala's mother, from the "The Story of the Boy Gopala" (See *Complete Works*, 5.168).

of, was there in Krishna, the Baby Cowherd, and all that heart entwined round the visible Cowherd, this little bronze image.[21]

Krishna talks of himself as God, as Christ does. He sees the Deity in himself. And he says, "None can go a day out of my path. All have to come to me. Whosoever wants to worship in whatsoever form, I give him faith in that form, and through that I meet him. ... " His heart is all for the masses.[22]

Pratyahara and *dharana*: Krishna says, "All who seek me by whatever means will reach me", "All must reach me." *Pratyahara* is a gathering toward, an attempt to get hold of the mind and focus it on the desired object. The first step is to let the mind drift; watch it; see what it thinks; be only the witness. Mind is not soul or spirit. It is only matter in a finer form, and we own it and can learn to manipulate it through the nerve energies.[23]

काङ्क्षन्तः कर्मणां सिद्धिं यजन्त इह देवताः ।
क्षिप्रं हि मानुषे लोके सिद्धिर्भवति कर्मजा ॥ १२ ॥

Longing for success in action, in this world, (people) worship the gods; because success resulting from action is quickly attained in the human world. —4. 12

They are good-natured, kind, and truthful. All is right with them, but that enjoyment is their God. It is a country where money flows like a river, with beauty as its ripple and learning its waves, and which rolls in luxury. "Longing for success in action, in this world, (men) worship the deities. For success is quickly attained through action in this world of man." Here you have a wonderful manifestation of grit and power—what strength, what practicality, and what manhood! Horses huge as elephants are drawing carriages that are as big as houses. You may take this as a specimen of the gigantic proportions in other things also. Here is a manifestation of tremendous energy.[24]

न मां कर्माणि लिम्पन्ति न मे कर्मफले स्पृहा ।
इति मां योऽभिजानाति कर्मभिर्न स बध्यते ॥ १४ ॥

Actions do not taint me, nor have I any thirst for the result
of action. He who knows me thus is not fettered by action.
—4. 14

एवं ज्ञात्वा कृतं कर्म पूर्वैरपि मुमुक्षुभिः ।
कुरु कर्मैव तस्मात् त्वं पूर्वैः पूर्वतरं कृतम् ॥ १५ ॥

Knowing thus, the ancient seekers after spiritual freedom
also performed action. Do thou, therefore, perform action
alone as did the ancients in olden times. —4. 15

"No action can touch me. I have no desire for the results of
action. Whosoever knows me thus knows the secret and is not
bound by action. The ancient sages, knowing this secret [could
safely engage in action]. Do thou work in the same fashion."[25]

किं कर्म किमकर्मेति कवयोऽप्यत्र मोहिताः ।
तत्ते कर्म प्रवक्ष्यामि यत् ज्ञात्वा मोक्ष्यसेऽशुभात् ॥ १६ ॥

Even sages are bewildered as to what is action and what is
inaction. I shall, therefore, tell you what action is, by knowing
which you will be freed from evil. —4. 16

In the Krishna Incarnation He says that the root of all sorts
of misery is *avidya* (nescience) and that selfless work purifies the
mind. But "Even sages are bewildered to decide what is work and
what is no-work." Only that kind of work which develops our
spirituality is work. Whatever fosters materiality is no-work.[26]

कर्मणो ह्यापि बोद्धव्यं बोद्धव्यं च विकर्मणः ।
अकर्मणश्च बोद्धव्यं गहना कर्मणो गतिः ॥ १७ ॥

For verily, (the true nature) even of karma or action should
be known, as also, that of *vikarma* or forbidden action, and

6

of *akarma* or inaction: the nature of karma is deep and impenetrable. —4. 17

Disciple: But, sir, if one has to renounce the fruits of work, why should one be induced to undertake work which is always troublesome?

Swamiji: In this human life, one cannot help doing some kind of work always. When man has perforce to do some work, *karma-yoga* enjoins on him to do it in such a way as will bring freedom through the realization of the Atman. As to your objection that none will be induced to work—the answer is, that whatever work you do has some motive behind it; but when by the long performance of work, one notices that one work merely leads to another, through a round of births and rebirths, then the awakened discrimination of man naturally begins to question itself, "Where is the end to this interminable chain of work?" It is then that he appreciates the full import of the words of the Lord in the Gita: "Inscrutable is the course of work." Therefore when the aspirant finds that work with motive brings no happiness, then he renounces action. But man is so constituted that to him the performance of work is a necessity, so what work should he take up? He takes up some unselfish work, but gives up all desire for its fruits. For he has known then that in those fruits of work lie countless seeds of future births and deaths. Therefore the knower of Brahman renounces all actions. Although to outward appearances he engages himself in some work, he has no attachment to it. Such men have been described in the scriptures as *karma-yogin*s.[27]

कर्मण्यकर्म यः पश्येद् अकर्मणि च कर्म यः ।
स बुद्धिमान् मनुष्येषु स युक्तः कृत्स्नकर्मकृत् ॥ १८ ॥

One who sees inaction in action, and action in inaction, is intelligent among human beings, he or she is a *yogi* and a doer of all action. —4. 18

Krishna preached in the midst of the battlefield. "He who in the midst of intense activity finds himself in the greatest calmness, and in the greatest peace finds intense activity, that is the greatest [*yogi* as well as the wisest man]."[28]

Everything goes to show that this philosophy must be very practical; and later on, when we come to the *Bhagavad Gita*—most of you, perhaps, have read it, it is the best commentary we have on the Vedanta philosophy—curiously enough the scene is laid on the battlefield, where Krishna teaches this philosophy to Arjuna; and the doctrine which stands out luminously in every page of the Gita is intense activity, but in the midst of it, eternal calmness. This is the secret of work, to attain which is the goal of the Vedanta. Inactivity, as we understand it in the sense of passivity, certainly cannot be the goal. Were it so, then the walls around us would be the most intelligent; they are inactive. Clods of earth, stumps of trees, would be the greatest sages in the world; they are inactive. Nor does inactivity become activity when it is combined with passion. Real activity, which is the goal of Vedanta, is combined with eternal calmness, the calmness which cannot be ruffled, the balance of mind which is never disturbed, whatever happens. And we all know from our experience in life that that is the best attitude for work.[29]

"He who sees in the midst of intense activity, intense calm, and in the midst of intensest peace is intensely active [is wise indeed]. ... This is the question: With every sense and every organ active, have you that tremendous peace [so that] nothing can disturb you? Standing on Market Street, waiting for the car with all the rush ... going on around you, are you in meditation—calm and peaceful? In the cave, are you intensely active there with all quiet about you? If you are, you are a *yogi*, otherwise not.[30]

The ideal man is he who, in the midst of the greatest silence and solitude, finds the intensest activity, and in the midst of the intensest activity finds the silence and solitude of the desert. He has learnt the secret of restraint, he has controlled himself. He goes through the streets of a big city with all its traffic, and his mind is as calm as if he were in a cave, where not a sound could reach him; and he is intensely working all the time. That is the ideal of *karma-yoga*, and if you have attained to that you have really learnt the secret of work.[31]

"He who in the midst of the greatest activity finds the sweetest peace, and in the midst of the greatest calmness is most active, he has known the secret of life." Krishna shows the way how to do this—by being non-attached: do everything but do not get identified with anything. You are the soul, the pure, the free, all the time; you are the Witness. Our misery comes, not from work, but by our getting attached to something.[32]

When we come to that non-attachment, then we can understand the marvellous mystery of the universe; how it is intense activity and vibration, and at the same time intensest peace and calm; how it is work every moment and rest every moment. That is the mystery of the universe—the impersonal and personal in one, the infinite and finite in one. Then we shall find the secret. "He who finds in the midst of intense activity the greatest rest, and in the midst of the greatest rest intense activity, he has become a *yogi*." He alone is a real worker, none else. We do a little work and break ourselves. Why? We become attached to that work. If we do not become attached, side by side with it we have infinite rest.[33]

Therefore Krishna teaches us not to shirk our duties, but to take them up manfully, and not think of the result. The servant has no right to question. The soldier has no right to reason. Go forward, and do not pay too much attention to the nature of the work you have to do. Ask your mind if you are unselfish. If you are, never mind anything, nothing can resist you! Plunge in! Do the duty at hand. And when you have done this, by degrees you will realize the Truth: "Whosoever in the midst of intense activity finds intense peace, whosoever in the midst of the greatest peace finds the greatest activity, he is a *yogi*, he is a great soul, he has arrived at perfection."[34]

Most of us cannot keep our activities on a par with our thought-lives. Some blessed ones can. Most of us seem to lose the power of work as we think deeper, and the power of deep thought if we work more. That is why most great thinkers have to leave to time the practical realization of their great ideals. Their thoughts must wait for more active brains to work them out and spread them. Yet, as we write, comes before us a vision of him, the charioteer of Arjuna, standing in his chariot between the contending hosts, his left hand curbing the fiery steeds—a mail-clad warrior, whose eagle-glance sweeps over the vast army, and as if by instinct weighs every detail of the battle array of both parties—at the same time that we hear, as it were, falling from his lips and thrilling the awe-struck Arjuna, that most marvellous secret of work: "He who finds rest in the midst of activity, and activity in rest, he is the wise amidst men, he the *yogi*, he is the doer of all work."[35]

Swamiji: A very funny thing happened today. I went to a friend's house. He has had a picture painted, the subject of which is "Shri Krishna addressing Arjuna on the battlefield of Kurukshetra". Shri Krishna stands on the chariot, holding the reins in His hand and preaching the Gita to Arjuna. He showed me the picture and asked me how I liked it. "Fairly well", I said. But as he insisted on having my criticism on it, I had to give my honest opinion by saying, "There is nothing in it to commend itself to me; first, because the chariot of the time of Shri Krishna was not like the modern pagoda-shaped car, and also, there is no expression in the figure of Shri Krishna."

Q.—How then should Shri Krishna be represented in the picture in question?

Swamiji: Shri Krishna ought to be painted as He really was, the Gita personified; and the central idea of the Gita should radiate from His whole form as He was teaching the path of dharma to Arjuna, who had been overcome by infatuation and cowardice.

So saying Swamiji posed himself in the way in which Shri Krishna should be portrayed, and continued: "Look here, thus does he hold the bridle of the horses—so tight that they are brought to their haunches, with their forelegs fighting the air, and their mouths gaping. This will show a tremendous play of action in the figure of Shri Krishna. His friend, the world-renowned hero, casting aside his bow and arrows, has sunk down like a coward on the chariot, in the midst of the two armies. And Shri Krishna, whip in one hand and tightening the reins with the other, has turned Himself towards Arjuna, with his childlike face beaming with unworldly love and sympathy, and a calm and serene look— and is delivering the message of the Gita to his beloved comrade. Now, tell me what idea this picture of the Preacher of the Gita conveys to you."

The friend: Activity combined with firmness and serenity.

Swamiji: Ay, that's it! Intense action in the whole body, and withal a face expressing the profound calmness and serenity of the blue sky. This is the central idea of the Gita—to be calm and steadfast in all circumstances, with one's body, mind, and soul centred at His hallowed Feet! ... He who even while doing action can keep his mind calm, and in whom, even when not doing any outward action, flows the current of activity in the form of the contemplation of Brahman, is the intelligent one among men, he indeed is the *yogi*, he indeed is the perfect worker.[36]

यस्य सर्वे समारम्भाः कामसङ्कल्पवर्जिताः ।
ज्ञानाग्नि दग्ध कर्माणं तमाहुः पण्डितं बुधाः ॥ १९ ॥

Whose undertakings are all devoid of *kama*, sensual desire, and *sankalpa*, desire for results, and whose actions are burnt by the fire of knowledge, him or her, the sages call wise. —4. 19

"[The seers call him wise] whose every attempt is free, without any desire for gain, without any selfishness." Truth can never come to us as long as we are selfish.[37]

We cannot remain without action for a moment. Act! But just as when your neighbour asks you, "Come and help me!" have you exactly the same idea when you are helping yourself? No more. Your body is of no more value than that of John. Don't do anything more for your body than you do for John. That is religion. "He whose efforts are bereft of all desire and selfishness has burnt all this bondage of action with the fire of knowledge. He is wise." Reading books cannot do that. The ass can be burdened with the whole library; that does not make him learned at all. What is the use of reading many books?[38]

त्यक्त्वा कर्मफलासङ्गं नित्यतृप्तो निराश्रयः ।
कर्मण्यभिप्रवृत्तोऽपि नैव किञ्चित् करोति सः ॥ २० ॥

Forsaking the clinging to fruits of action, ever satisfied, depending on nothing, even though engaged in action, he or she does not really do anything. —4. 20

"Giving up all attachment to work, always satisfied, not hoping for gain, the wise man acts and is beyond action."[39]

श्रेयान् द्रव्यमयात् यज्ञात् ज्ञानयज्ञः परन्तप ।
सर्वं कर्माखिलं पार्थ ज्ञाने परिसमाप्यते ॥ ३३ ॥

Knowledge-sacrifice, O scorcher of foes, is superior to sacrifice (performed) with (material) objects; all action, in its entirety, O Partha, attains its consummation in knowledge. —4. 33

As to the so-called Hindu idolatry—first go and learn the forms they are going through, and where it is that the worshippers are really worshipping, whether in the temple, in the image, or in the temple of their own bodies. First know for certain what they are doing—which more than ninety per cent of the revilers are thoroughly ignorant of—and then it will explain itself in the light of the Vedantic philosophy. Still these karmas are not compulsory. On the other hand, open your Manu and see where it orders every old man to embrace the fourth *ashrama*, and whether he embraces it or not, he must give up all karma. It is reiterated everywhere that all these karmas "finally end in *jnana*".[40]

Disciple: Sir, now you are speaking of *jnana*; but sometimes you proclaim the superiority of *bhakti*, sometimes of karma, and sometimes of yoga. This confuses our understanding.

Swamiji: Well, the truth is this. The knowledge of Brahman is the ultimate goal—the highest destiny of man. But man cannot remain absorbed in Brahman all the time. When he comes out of it, he must have something to engage himself. At that time he should do such work as will contribute to the real well-being of people. Therefore do I urge you in the service of *jivas** in a spirit of oneness. But, my son, such are the intricacies of work, that even great saints are caught in them and become attached. Therefore work has to be done without any desire for results. This is the teaching of the Gita. But know that in the knowledge of Brahman there is no touch of any relation to work. Good works, at the most, purify the mind. Therefore has the commentator Shankara so sharply criticized the doctrine of the combination of *jnana* and karma. Some attain to the knowledge of Brahman by the means of unselfish work. This is also a means, but the end is the realization of Brahman. Know this thoroughly that the goal of the path of discrimination and of all other modes of practice is the realization of Brahman.[41]

---

* The living beings.

तद् विद्धि प्रणिपातेन परिप्रश्नेन सेवया ।
उपदेक्ष्यन्ति ते ज्ञानं ज्ञानिनः तत्त्वदर्शिनः ॥ ३४॥

Know That (supreme Brahman), by prostrating yourself, by repeated questioning, and by service; the *jnanis*, those who have realized the Truth, will instruct you in that knowledge. —4. 34

Swamiji began to speak to the disciple [Sharat Chandra Chakravarty], enjoining him to be reverential to the Math members: "These children of Shri Ramakrishna whom you see, are wonderful *tyagis* (selfless souls), and by service to them you will attain to the purification of mind and be blessed with the vision of the Atman. You remember the words of the Gita: 'By interrogation and service to the great soul'. Therefore you must serve them, by which you will attain your goal; and you know how much they love you."[42]

न हि ज्ञानेन सदृशं पवित्रमिह विद्यते ।
तत्स्वयं योगसंसिद्धः कालेनात्मनि विन्दति ॥ ३८॥

Verily, there exists nothing in this world as purifying as *jnana* or spiritual knowledge. In good time, having reached perfection in yoga, one realizes that in oneself. —4. 38

It has been said that adversity is the touchstone of true knowledge, and this may be said a hundred times with regard to the truth: "Thou art That." This truly diagnoses the *vairagya* (dispassion) disease. Blessed is the life of one who has developed this symptom. In spite of your dislike I repeat the old saying: "Wait for a short time." You are tired with rowing; rest on your oars. The momentum will take the boat to the other side. This has been said in the Gita, "In good time, having reached perfection in yoga, one realizes That in one's own heart."[43]

Disciple: It is a matter of deep regret that even hearing this from you almost every day, I have not been able to realize it.

Swamiji: Renunciation must come, but in the fullness of time. "In the fullness of time one attains to knowledge within himself." When the few *samskaras* (tendencies) of the previous life are spent, then renunciation sprouts up in the heart.[44]

अज्ञश्च अश्रद्दधानश्च संशयात्मा विनश्यति ।
नायं लोकोऽस्ति न परो न सुखं संशयात्मनः ॥ ४० ॥

The ignorant person, the person without *shraddha*, the doubting self, goes to destruction. The doubting self has neither this world nor the next nor happiness. —4. 40

Likewise the education that our boys receive is very negative. The schoolboy learns nothing, but has everything of his own broken down—want of *shraddha* is the result. The *shraddha* which is the keynote of the Veda and the Vedanta—the *shraddha* which emboldened Nachiketa to face Yama and question him, through which *shraddha* this world moves—the annihilation of that *shraddha*! "The ignorant, the man devoid of *shraddha*, the doubting self runs to ruin." Therefore are we so near to destruction. The remedy now is the spread of education.[45]

CHAPTER V

ज्ञेय: स नित्यसंन्यासी यो न द्वेष्टि न कांक्षति ।
निर्द्वन्द्वो हि महाबाहो सुखं बन्धात् प्रमुच्यते ॥ ३ ॥

He or she should be known a constant *sannyasi*, who has no personal likes, nor dislikes; for, free from the pairs of opposites, O mighty armed, that person is easily set free from bondage. —5. 3

The whole world is a mere child's play—preaching, teaching, and all included. "Know him to be the *sannyasin* who neither hates not desires." And what is there to be desired in this little mud-puddle of a world, with its ever-recurring misery, disease, and death? "He who has given up all desires, he alone is happy."[1]

सांख्ययोगौ पृथग्बाला: प्रवदन्ति न पण्डिता: ।
एकं अपि आस्थित: सम्यक् उभयोर्विन्दते फलम् ॥ ४ ॥

Childlike or immature people, not the wise, speak of Self-knowledge and yoga of action, as distinct; one who is truly established in one, gains the fruits of both. —5. 4

The yogas of work, of wisdom, and of devotion are all capable of serving as direct and independent means for the attainment of *moksha*. "Fools alone say that work and philosophy are different, not the learned." The learned know that, though apparently different from each other, they at last lead to the same goal of human perfection.[2]

ब्रह्मण्याधाय कर्माणि सङ्गं त्यक्त्वा करोति यः ।
लिप्यते न स पापेन पद्मपत्रं इवाम्भसा ॥ १० ॥

One who does actions forsaking attachment, resigning them
to Brahman, is not tainted by evil, like a lotus-leaf by water.
—5. 10

"Whosoever lives in the midst of the world, and works, and
gives up all the fruit of his action unto the Lord, he is never
touched with the evils of the world. Just as the lotus, born under
the water, rises up and blossoms above the water, even so is the
man who is engaged in the activities of the world, giving up all
the fruit of his activities unto the Lord."[3]

He [Krishna] taught that a man ought to live in this world
like a lotus leaf, which grows in water but is never moistened by
water; so a man ought to live in the world—his heart to God and
his hands to work.[4]

The aim and end in this life for the *jnana-yogi* is to become
this *jivanmukta*, "living-free". He is *jivanmukta* who can live in
this world without being attached. He is like the lotus leaves in
water, which are never wetted by the water.[5]

The Lord Himself works incessantly and is ever without
attachment. Just as water cannot wet the lotus leaf, so work
cannot bind the unselfish man by giving rise to attachment to
results. The selfless and unattached man may live in the very heart
of a crowded and sinful city; he will not be touched by sin.[6]

So *karma-yoga* says, first destroy the tendency to project this
tentacle of selfishness, and when you have the power of checking
it, hold it in and do not allow the mind to get into the ways of
selfishness. Then you may go out into the world and work as much
as you can. Mix everywhere, go where you please; you will never
be contaminated with evil. There is the lotus leaf in the water; the
water cannot touch and adhere to it; so will you be in the world.
This is called *vairagya*, dispassion or non-attachment. I believe I

have told you that without non-attachment there cannot be any kind of yoga. Non-attachment is the basis of all the yogas.[7]

कायेन मनसा बुद्ध्या केवलैरिन्द्रियैरपि ।
योगिनः कर्म कुर्वन्ति सङ्गं त्यक्त्वात्मशुद्धये ॥ ११ ॥

Following the yoga of work, *yogi*s perform action only with body, mind, senses and intellect, forsaking attachment, for the purification of the heart. —5. 11

Disciple: But, sir, since the obstacles to Self-manifestation are not overcome without the performance of work in some form or other, therefore indirectly work stands as a means to knowledge.

Swamiji: From the standpoint of the causal chain, it so appears prima facie. Taking up this view it is stated in the Purva-Mimamsa that work for a definite end infallibly produces a definite result. But the vision of the Atman which is Absolute is not to be compassed by means of work. For the rule with regard to a seeker of the Atman is that he should undergo spiritual practice, but have no eye to its results. It follows thence that these practices are simply the cause of the purification of the aspirant's mind. For if the Atman could be directly realized as a result of these practices, then scriptures would not have enjoined on the aspirant to give up the results of work. So it is with a view to combating the Purva-Mimamsa doctrine of work with motive producing results, that the philosophy of work without motive has been set forth in the Gita. Do you see?[8]

युक्तः कर्मफलं त्यक्त्वा शान्तिं आप्नोति नैष्ठिकीम् ।
अयुक्तः कामकारेण फले सक्तो निबध्यते ॥ १२ ॥

The well-poised one, forsaking the fruit of action, attains peace, born of steadfastness; the unbalanced one, led by desire, is bound by being attached to the fruits (of action). —5. 12

We read in the *Bhagavad Gita* again and again that we must all work incessantly. All work is by nature composed of good and evil. We cannot do any work which will not do some good somewhere; there cannot be any work which will not cause some harm somewhere. Every work must necessarily be a mixture of good and evil; yet we are commanded to work incessantly. Good and evil will both have their results, will produce their karma. Good action will entail upon us good effect; bad action, bad. But good and bad are both bondages of the soul. The solution reached in the Gita in regard to this bondage-producing nature of work is that, if we do not attach ourselves to the work we do, it will not have any binding effect on our soul.[9]

विद्या विनय संपन्ने ब्राह्मणे गवि हस्तिनि ।
शुनि चैव श्वपाके च पण्डिताः समदर्शिनः ॥ १८ ॥

The *pandita*s or knowers of the Self look with an equal eye on a *brahmana* endowed with learning and humility, a cow, an elephant, a dog, and an eater of dogs (low-caste person). —5.18

Those of you who have studied the Gita will remember the memorable passages: "He who looks upon the learned Brahmin, upon the cow, the elephant, the dog, or the outcast with the same eye, he indeed is the sage, and the wise man."[10]

The real Vedantist alone will give up his life for a fellow-man without any compunction, because he knows he will not die. As long as there is one insect left in the world, he is living; as long as one mouth eats, he eats. So he goes on doing good to others; and is never hindered by the modern ideas of caring for the body. When a man reaches this point of abnegation, he goes beyond the moral struggle, beyond everything. He sees in the most learned priest, in the cow, in the dog, in the most miserable places, neither the learned man, nor the cow, nor the dog, nor the miserable place, but the same divinity manifesting itself in them all. He alone is the happy man; and the man who has acquired that sameness has, even in this life, conquered all existence.[11]

Last of all will come self-surrender. Then we shall be able to give ourselves up to the Mother. If misery comes, welcome; if happiness comes, welcome. Then, when we come up to this love, all crooked things shall be straight. There will be the same sight for the Brahmin, the Pariah, and the dog. Until we love the universe with same-sightedness, with impartial, undying love, we are missing again and again. But then all will have vanished, and we shall see in all the same infinite eternal Mother.[12]

इहैव तैर्जितः सर्गो येषां साम्ये स्थितं मनः ।
निर्दोषं हि समं ब्रह्म तस्माद् ब्रह्मणि ते स्थिताः ॥ १९ ॥

(Relative) existence has been conquered by them, even in this world, whose mind rests in sameness, since Brahman is the same in all and is without imperfection; therefore, they indeed rest in Brahman. —5. 19

Breaking the bondages of all, the chains of all, declaring liberty to all to reach the highest goal, come the words of the Gita, rolls like thunder the mighty voice of Krishna: "Even in this life they have conquered relativity, whose minds are firmly fixed upon the sameness, for God is pure and the same to all, therefore such are said to be living in God."[13]

"Even in this life he has conquered relative existence whose mind is firmly fixed on this sameness, for the Lord is one and the same to all, and the Lord is pure; therefore those who have this sameness for all, and are pure, are said to be living in God." This is the gist of Vedantic morality—this sameness for all.[14]

Therefore the absolute sameness of conditions, if that be the aim of ethics, appears to be impossible. That all men should be the same, could never be, however we might try. Men will be born differentiated; some will have more power than others; some will have natural capacities, others not; some will have perfect bodies, others not. We can never stop that. At the same time ring in our ears the wonderful words of morality proclaimed by various teachers: "Thus, seeing the same God equally present in all, the sage does not injure Self by the Self, and thus reaches the highest goal. Even in this life they have conquered relative existence whose minds are firmly fixed on this sameness; for God is pure, and God is the same to all. Therefore such are said to be living in God." We cannot deny that this is the real idea; yet at the same time comes the difficulty that the sameness as regards external forms and position can never be attained.[15]

Dualism is the natural idea of the senses; as long as we are bound by the senses we are bound to see a God who is only Personal, and nothing but Personal, we are bound to see the world as it is. Says Ramanuja, "So long as you think you are a body, and you think you are a mind, and you think you are a *jiva*, every act of perception will give you the three—Soul, and nature, and something as causing both." But yet, at the same time, even the idea of the body disappears where the mind itself becomes finer and finer, till it has almost disappeared, when all the different things that make us fear, make us weak, and bind us down to this body-life have disappeared. Then and then alone one finds out the truth of that grand old teaching. What is the teaching? "Even in this life they have conquered the round of birth and death whose minds are firm-fixed on the sameness of everything, for God is pure and the same to all, and therefore such are said to be living in God."[16]

But above all, let me once more remind you that here is need of practical work, and the first part of that is that you should go to the sinking millions of India, and take them by the hand, remembering the words of the Lord Krishna: "Even in this life they have conquered relative existence whose minds are firm-fixed on the sameness of everything, for God is pure and the same to all; therefore, such are said to be living in God."[17]

This is what one of your ancestors said: "Even in this life, they have conquered relativity whose mind is fixed in sameness"—one who is believed to be God incarnate. We all believe it. Are his words then vain and without meaning? If not, and we know they are not, any attempt against this perfect equality of all creation, irrespective of birth, sex, or even qualification, is a terrible mistake, and no one can be saved until he has attained to this idea of sameness. Follow, therefore, noble Prince,* the teachings of the Vedanta, not as explained by this or that commentator, but as the Lord within you understands them. Above all, follow this great doctrine of sameness in all things, through all beings, seeing the same God in all. This is the way to freedom; inequality, the way to bondage. No man and no nation can attempt to gain physical freedom without physical equality, nor mental freedom without mental equality. Ignorance, inequality, and desire are the three causes of human misery, and each follows the other in inevitable union. Why should a man think himself above any other man, or even an animal? It is the same throughout: "त्वं स्त्री त्वं पुमानसि त्वं कुमार उत वा कुमारि—Thou art the man, Thou the woman, Thou art the young man, Thou the young woman." Many will say, "That is all right for the *sannyasins*, but we are householders." No doubt, a householder having many other duties to perform, cannot as fully attain to this sameness; yet this should be also their ideal, for it is the ideal of all societies, of all mankind, all animals, and all nature, to attain to this sameness.[18]

The *yogi* says, every man is a slave except the *yogi*. He is a slave of food, to air, to his wife, to his children, to a dollar, slave to a nation, slave to name and fame, and to a thousand things in this world. The man who is not controlled by any one of these bondages is alone a real man, a real *yogi*. "They have conquered relative existence in this life who are firm-fixed in sameness. God is pure and the same to all. Therefore such are said to be living in God."[19]

"They indeed have conquered Heaven even in this life whose mind has become fixed in sameness. God is pure and same to

* The Raja of Khetri.

all, therefore they are said to be in God." Desire, ignorance, and inequality—this is the trinity of bondage. Denial of the will to live, knowledge, and same-sightedness is the trinity of liberation.[20]

CHAPTER VI

उद्धरेत् आत्मनात्मानं नात्मानं अवसादयेत् ।
आत्मैव ह्यात्मनो बन्धुरात्मैव रिपुरात्मनः ॥ ५ ॥

Raise yourself by yourself; don't let yourself down, for you alone are your own friend, you alone are your own enemy.
—6. 5

"Deliver thou thyself by thyself! Ah, do not let thyself sink! For thou art thyself thy greatest friend. And thou thyself thy greatest enemy."[1]

"One must save the self by one's own self"—by personal prowess.[2]

It is a tremendous error to feel helpless. Do not seek help from anyone. We are our own help. If we cannot help ourselves, there is none to help us. "Thou thyself art thy only friend, thou thyself thy only enemy. There is no other enemy but this self of mine, no other friend by myself." This is the last and greatest lesson, and Oh, what a time it takes to learn it! We seem to get hold of it, and the next moment the old wave comes. The backbone breaks. We weaken and again grasp for that superstition and help. Just think of that huge mass of misery, and all caused by this false idea of going to seek for help![3]

Be not afraid. Think not how many times you fail. Never mind. Time is infinite. Go forward; assert yourself again and again, and light must come. You may pray to everyone that was ever born, but who will come to help you? And what of the way of death from which none knows escape? Help thyself out by thyself. None else can help thee, friend. For thou alone art thy greatest enemy, thou alone art thy greatest friend. Get hold of the Self, then. Stand up. Don't be afraid.[4]

There is no help for man. None ever was, none is, and none will be. Why should there be? Are you not men and women? Are the lords of the earth to be helped by others? Are you not ashamed? You will be helped when you are reduced to dust. But you are spirit. Pull yourself out of difficulties by yourself! Save yourself by yourself! There is none to help you—never was. To think that there is, is sweet delusion. It comes to no good.[5]

"One should raise the self by the self." Let each one work out one's own salvation. Freedom in all matters, i.e. advance towards *mukti* is the worthiest gain of man. To advance oneself towards freedom—physical, mental, and spiritual—and help others to do so, is the supreme prize of man. Those social rules which stand in the way of the unfoldment of this freedom are injurious, and steps should be taken to destroy them speedily. Those institutions should be encouraged by which men advance in the path of freedom.[6]

Teach some boys and girls of the peasant classes the rudiments of learning and infuse a number of ideas into their brains. Afterwards the peasants of each village will collect funds and have one of these in their village. "One must raise oneself by one's own exertions"—this holds good in all spheres. We help them to help themselves. That they are supplying you with your daily bread is a real bit of work done. The moment they will come to understand their own condition and feel the necessity of help and improvement, know that your work is taking effect and is in the right direction.[7]

They tried, and they failed. Why? Because few of them ever studied their own religion, and not one ever underwent the training necessary to understand the Mother of all religions. I claim that no destruction of religion is necessary to improve the Hindu society, and that this state of society exists not on account of religion, but because religion has not been applied to society as it should have been. This I am ready to prove from our old books, every word of it. This is what I teach, and this is what we must struggle all our lives to carry out. But it will take time, a long time to study. Have patience and work. ... Save yourself by yourself.[8]

ज्ञान विज्ञान तृप्तात्मा कूटस्थो विजितेन्द्रियः ।
युक्त इत्युच्यते योगी समलोष्टाश्मकाञ्चनः ॥ ८ ॥

Whose heart is filled with satisfaction through knowledge and wisdom, and is steady, whose senses are conquered, and to whom a lump of earth, stone, and gold are the same, that *yogi* is called steadfast. —6. 8

There are many passages in the *Dhammapada* too, with similar ideas. But that is at the last stage when one has got perfectly satisfied with knowledge and realization, is the same under all circumstances and has gained mastery over his senses— "ज्ञान विज्ञान तृप्तात्मा कूटस्थो विजितेन्द्रियः". He who has not the least regard for his body as something to be taken care of—it is he who may roam about at pleasure like the mad elephant caring for naught. Whereas a puny creature like myself should practice devotion, sitting at one spot, till he attains realization; and then only should he behave like that; but it is a far-off question—very far indeed.[9]

नात्यश्नतस्तु योगोऽस्ति न चैकान्तमनश्नतः ।
न चातिस्वप्नशीलस्य जाग्रतो नैव चार्जुन ॥ १६ ॥

(Success in) yoga is not for the person who eats too much or does not eat at all for long periods; nor, O Arjuna, for one who sleeps too much or keeps awake for long. —6. 16

A *yogi* must avoid the two extremes of luxury and austerity. He must not fast, nor torture his flesh. He who does so, says the Gita, cannot be a *yogi*: He who fasts, he who keeps awake, he who sleeps much, he who works too much, he who does no work, none of these can be a *yogi*.[10]

The food must be simple and taken several times [a day] instead of once or twice. Never get very hungry. "He who eats too much cannot be a *yogi*. He who fasts too much cannot be a *yogi*. He who sleeps too much cannot be a *yogi*, nor he who keeps awake too much." He who does not do any work and he who works too hard cannot succeed. Proper food, proper exercise, proper sleep, proper wakefulness—these are necessary for any success.[11]

The body must be properly taken care of. The people who torture their flesh are demoniacal. Always keep your mind joyful; if melancholy thoughts come, kick them out. A *yogi* must not eat too much, but he also must not fast; he must not sleep too much, but he must not go without any sleep. In all things only the man who holds the golden mean can become a *yogi*.[12]

The explanation of nature is in us; the stone falls outside, but gravitation is in us, not outside. Those who stuff themselves, those who starve themselves, those who sleep too much, those who sleep too little, cannot become *yogi*s. Ignorance, fickleness, jealousy, laziness, and excessive attachment are the great enemies to success in yoga practice.[13]

यं लब्ध्वा चापरं लाभं मन्यते नाधिकं ततः ।
यस्मिन्स्थितो न दुःखेन गुरुणापि विचाल्यते ॥ २२॥

Having obtained which, one regards no other acquisition superior to that, and where established, one is not moved even by heavy sorrow. —6. 22*

"Established in which state a man is not moved even by great misfortune."[14]

---

* Swamiji quoted the last half of this verse in a letter to Swami Rama-krishnananda.

सर्वभूतस्थं आत्मानं सर्वभूतानि चात्मनि ।
ईक्षते योगयुक्तात्मा सर्वत्र समदर्शनः ॥ २९ ॥

With the heart concentrated by yoga, with the eye of evenness for all things, he or she beholds the Self in all beings and all beings in the Self. —6. 29

What is the reason that I should be moral? You cannot explain it except when you come to know the truth as given in the Gita: "He who sees everyone in himself, and himself in everyone, the sage does not injure the Self by the self.[15]

The first end of life is knowledge; the second end of life is happiness. Knowledge and happiness lead to freedom. But not one can attain liberty until every being (ant or dog) has liberty. Not one can be happy until all are happy. When you hurt anyone you hurt yourself, for you and your brother are one. He is indeed a *yogi* who sees himself in the whole universe and the whole universe in himself. Self-sacrifice, not self-assertion, is the law of the highest universe. The world is so evil because Jesus' teaching, "Resist not evil", has never been tried. Selflessness alone will solve the problem. Religion comes with intense self-sacrifice. Desire nothing for yourself. Do all for others. This is to live and move and have your being in God.[16]

असंशयं महाबाहो मनो दुर्निग्रहं चलम् ।
अभ्यासेन तु कौन्तेय वैराग्येण च गृह्यते ॥३५॥

Without doubt, O mighty-armed, the mind is restless and difficult to control; but through practice and renunciation, O son of Kunti, it can be achieved. —6. 35

"Only by practice and non-attachment can we conquer mind."[17]

To restrain the *indriya*s (organs) from going towards the objects of the senses, to control them and bring them under the guidance of the will, is the very central virtue in religious culture.

Then comes the practice of self-restraint and self-denial. All the immense possibilities of divine realization in the soul cannot get actualized without struggle and without such practice on the part of the aspiring devotee. "The mind must always think of the Lord." It is very hard at first to compel the mind to think of the Lord always, but with every new effort the power to do so grows stronger in us. "By practice, O son of Kunti, and by non-attachment is it attained", says Shri Krishna in the Gita.[18]

Disciple: Sir, it is so difficult to direct this uncontrolled mind towards Brahman.

Swamiji: Is there anything difficult for the hero? Only men of faint hearts speak so. "वीराणामेव करतलगता मुक्ति: न पुन: कापुरुषाणाम्— *Mukti* is easy of attainment only to the hero—but not to cowards." Says the Gita, "By renunciation and by practice is the mind brought under control, O Arjuna." The *chitta* or mind-stuff is like a transparent lake, and the waves which rise in it by the impact of sense-impressions constitute *manas* or the mind. Therefore the mind consists of a succession of thought-waves. From these mental waves arises desire. Then that desire transforms itself into will and works through its gross instrument, the body. Again, as work is endless, so its fruits also are endless. Hence the mind is always being tossed by countless myriads of waves—the fruits of work. This mind has to be divested of all modifications (*vrittis*) and reconverted into the transparent lake, so that there remains not a single wave of modification in it. Then will Brahman manifest Itself.[19]

पार्थ नैवेह नामुत्र विनाश: तस्य विद्यते ।
नहि कल्याणकृत् कश्चित् दुर्गतिं तात गच्छति ।। ४० ।।

Verily, O son of Pritha, there is no destruction for such a one, neither here nor hereafter, for, the doer of good, O my son, never comes to grief. —6. 40

CHAPTER VI

[The following paragraph is a reminiscence by Swami Vivekananda's disciple Sharat Chandra Chakravarty.]

At the time Belur Math was established, many among the
orthodox Hindus were wont to make sharp criticism of the ways
of life in the Math. Hearing the report of such criticism from
the disciple, Swamiji would say (in the words of the couplet
of Tulasidas), "The elephant passes in the market-place, and a
thousand curs begin barking after him; so the *sadhu*s have no ill-
feeling when worldly people slander them." Or again he would
say, "Without persecution no beneficent idea can enter into the
heart of a society." He would exhort everybody, "Go on working
without an eye to results. One day you are sure to reap the fruits of
it." Again, on the lips of Swamiji were very often heard the words
of the Gita, "A doer of good never comes to grief, my son."[20]

In reference to me every now and then attacks are made in
missionary papers (so I hear), but I never care to see them. If you
send any of those made in India, I should throw them into the
wastepaper basket. A little agitation was necessary for our work.
We have had enough. Pay no more attention to what people
say about me, whether good or bad. You go on with your work
and remember that "Never one meets with evil who tries to do
good."[21]

Disciple: But where is that strength in us? I should have felt
myself blessed if I had a hundredth part of your powers, Swamiji.

Swamiji: How foolish! Power and things like that will come
by themselves. Put yourself to work, and you will find such
tremendous power coming to you that you will find it hard to
bear. Even the least work done for others awakens the power
within; even thinking the least good of others gradually instils
into the heart the strength of a lion. I love you all ever so much,
but I wish you all to die working for others—I should rather be
glad to see you do that!

Disciple: What will become of those, then, who depend on me?

Swamiji: If you are ready to sacrifice your life for others, God will certainly provide some means for them. Have you not read in the Gita the words of Shri Krishna, "Never does a doer of good, O my beloved, come to grief?"[22]

Disciple: Sir, to start Feeding Homes we want a site first, then buildings, and then the funds to work them. Where will so much money come from?

Swamiji: The southern portion of the Math premises I am leaving at your disposal immediately, and I am getting a thatched house erected under that *bael* tree. You just find out one or two blind or infirm people and apply yourself to their service. Go and beg food for them yourself; cook with your own hands and feed them. If you continue this for some days, you will find that lots of people will be coming forward to assist you with plenty of money. "Never, my son, does a doer of good come to grief."[23]

Duty has no end, and the world is extremely selfish. Be of good cheer. "Never a worker of good came to grief."[24]

तत्र तं बुद्धिसंयोगं लभते पौर्वदेहिकम् ।
यतते च ततो भूयः संसिद्धौ कुरुनन्दन ॥ ४३ ॥

There, one is united with the intelligence acquired in the former body, and strives more than before, for perfection, O son of the Kurus. —6. 43

But though it is so hard to reach the goal, yet even our smallest attempts are not in vain. We know that nothing is lost. In the Gita, Arjuna asks Krishna*, "Those who fail in attaining perfection in yoga in this life, are they destroyed like the clouds of summer?" Krishna replies, "Nothing, my friend, is lost in this world. Whatever one does, that remains as one's own, and if the

---

* Gita, 6.38.

fruition of yoga does not come in this life, one takes it up again in the next birth." Otherwise, how do you explain the marvellous childhood of Jesus, Buddha, Shankara?[25]

प्रयत्नाद्यतमानस्तु योगी संशुद्धकिल्बिषः ।
अनेकजन्म संसिद्धः ततो याति परां गतिम् ॥ ४५ ॥

The *yogi*, striving assiduously, purified of taint, gradually gaining perfection through many births, then reaches the highest goal. —6. 45

Just take your own case—do you think it is possible without the grace of God to have the blessed company of Nag Mahashaya, a man who rose to spiritual perfection through the strength of divine grace and came to know fully what this grace really means? "One attains the highest stage after being perfected by the practice of repeated births." It is only by virtue of great religious merit acquired through many births that one comes across a great soul like him. All the characteristics of the highest type of *bhakti*, spoken of in the scriptures, have manifested themselves in Nag Mahashaya. It is only in him that we actually see fulfilled the widely quoted text, तृणादपि सुनीचेन.* Blessed indeed is your East Bengal to have been hallowed by the touch of Nag Mahashaya's feet![26]

---

* "Lowlier far than the lowly stalk of grass."

CHAPTER VII

मनुष्याणां सहस्रेषु कश्चित् यतति सिद्धये ।
यततां अपि सिद्धानां कश्चित् मां वेत्ति तत्त्वतः ॥ ३ ॥

A few, among thousands of men and women, strive for
perfection; and a few perchance, among the blessed ones
striving thus, know Me in reality. —7. 3

Very few men ask for the truth, fewer dare to learn the truth,
and fewest of all dare to follow it in all its practical bearings. It is
not their fault; it is all weakness of the brain.[1]

I feel as if I had my share of experience in what they call
"work". I am finished, I am longing now to get out. "Out of
thousands, but one strives to attain the Goal. And even of those
who struggle hard, but few attain"; for the senses are powerful,
they drag men down.[2]

मत्तः परतरं नान्यत् किञ्चिदस्ति धनञ्जय ।
मयि सर्वमिदं प्रोतं सूत्रे मणिगणा इव ॥ ७ ॥

Beyond me, O Dhananjaya (Arjuna), there is nothing higher.
All this is strung in Me, like a row of pearls on a thread. —7. 7

It is the same light coming through glasses of different
colours. And these little variations are necessary for purposes
of adaptation. But in the heart of everything the same truth
reigns. The Lord has declared to the Hindu in His incarnation
as Krishna, "I am in every religion as the thread through a string
of pearls."[3]

So it is with this universal religion, which runs through all
the various religions of the world in the form of God; it must and

does exist through eternity. "I am the thread that runs through all these pearls," and each pearl is a religion or even a sect thereof. Such are the different pearls, and the Lord is the thread that runs through all of them; only the majority of mankind are entirely unconscious of it.[4]

In the Gita we already hear the distant sound of the conflicts of sects, and the Lord comes in the middle to harmonize them all; He, the great preacher of harmony, the greatest teacher of harmony, Lord Shri Krishna. He says, "In Me they are all strung like pearls upon a thread."[5]

[To a request of the *New York World* of October 1, 1893, for "a sentiment or expression regarding the significance of the great meeting" from each representative, Swamiji replied with the quotations given in the following paragraph; one quotation is from the Gita and one from Vyasa.]

"I am He that am in every religion—like the thread that passes through a string of pearls." "Holy, perfect and pure men are seen in all creeds, therefore they all lead to the same truth—for how can nectar be the outcome of poison?"[6]

The idea of the cruel and ruthless Jehovah in the *Old Testament* has frightened many—but why? What right have they to assume that the Jehovah of the ancient Jews must represent the conventional idea of the God of the present day? At the same time, we must not forget that there will come men after us who will laugh at our ideas of religion and God in the same way that we laugh at those of the ancients. Yet, through all these various conceptions runs the golden thread of unity, and it is the purpose of the Vedanta to discover this thread. "I am the thread that runs through all these various ideas, each one of which is like a pearl," says the Lord Krishna; and it is the duty of Vedanta to establish this connecting thread, however incongruous or disgusting may seem these ideas when judged according to the conceptions of today. These ideas, in the setting of past times, were harmonious and not more hideous than our present ideas. It is only when we try to take them out of their settings and apply to our present circumstances that the hideousness becomes obvious. For the old surroundings are dead and gone. Just as the ancient Jew has developed into the keen, modern, sharp Jew, and the ancient Aryan into the intellectual Hindu, similarly Jehovah has grown, and Devas have grown.[7]

दैवी ह्येषा गुणमयी मम माया दुरत्यया ।
मामेव ये प्रपद्यन्ते मायां एतां तरन्ति ते ॥ १४ ॥

Verily, this Maya of Mine, constituted of the *guna*s, is difficult to cross over; those who devote themselves to Me alone, cross over this illusion. —7. 14

We find that with all this, with this terrible fact before us, in the midst of sorrow and suffering, even in this world where life and death are synonymous, even here, there is a still small voice that is ringing through all ages, through every country, and in every heart: "This My Maya is divine, made up of qualities, and very difficult to cross. Yet those that come unto Me, cross the river of life." "Come unto Me all ye that labour and are heavy laden, and I will give you rest." This is the voice that is leading us forward. Man has heard it, and is hearing it all through the ages. This voice comes to men when everything seems to be lost and hope has fled, when man's dependence on his own strength has been crushed down, and everything seems to melt away between his fingers, and life is a hopeless ruin. Then he hears it. This is called religion.[8]

We have to come to this idea: "This My Maya is divine." It is My activity [My] divinity. "[My Maya] is hard to cross, but those that take refuge in me [go beyond Maya]." But you find out that it is very difficult to cross this ocean [of Maya by] yourself. You cannot. It is the old question—hen and egg. If you do any work, that work becomes the cause and produces the effect. That effect [again] becomes the cause and produces the effect. And so on. If you push this down, it never stops. Once you set a thing in motion, there is no more stopping. I do some work, good or bad, [and it sets up a chain reaction] … I cannot stop now. It is impossible for us to get out from this bondage [by ourselves]. It is only possible if there is someone more powerful than this law of causation, and if he takes mercy on us and drags us out. And we declare that there is such a one—god. There is such a being, all merciful.[9]

"He that followeth Me, walketh not in darkness", saith the Lord [John 8.12].[10] (*The Imitation of Christ*, V.1.)*

चतुर्विधा भजन्ते मां जनाः सुकृतिनोऽर्जुन ।
आर्तो जिज्ञासुः अर्थार्थी ज्ञानी च भरतर्षभ ॥ १६ ॥

Four kinds of virtuous human beings worship Me, O Arjuna—the distressed, the seeker of knowledge, the seeker of wealth, and the spiritually wise, O bull (greatest) among the Bharatas. —7. 16

तेषां ज्ञानी नित्ययुक्त एकभक्तिः विशिष्यते ।
प्रियो हि ज्ञानिनोऽत्यर्थं अहं स च मम प्रियः ॥ १७ ॥

Of them, the *jnani*, the wise person, ever-steadfast, (and fired) with devotion to the One, excels; for supremely dear am I to the *jnani*, and he or she also is dear to Me. —7. 17

Four sorts of people worship Me. Some want the delights of the physical world. Some want money, some want religion. Some worship Me because they love Me. Real love is love for love's sake. I do not ask health or money or life or salvation. Send me

---

*This passage is the English version of Swami Vivekananda's translation of *The Imitation of Christ* (V. 1) into Bengali. To this he had supplied the following footnote referring to the Gita (7. 14): This My Maya is divine, made up of qualities and very difficult to cross. Yet those who come unto Me, cross the river of life.

to a thousand hells, but let me love Thee for love's sake. Mira Bai, the great queen, taught the doctrine of love for love's sake.[11]

Miserable are the diseased people; they are great worshippers of the Lord, for they hope that if they pray to Him He will heal them. Not that that is altogether bad—if such prayers are honest and if they remember that that is not religion. Shri Krishna says in the Gita, "Four classes of people worship Me: the distressed, the seeker of material things, the inquirer, and the knower of truth." People who are in distress approach God for relief. If they are ill, they worship Him to be healed; if they lose their wealth, they pray to Him to get it back. There are other people who ask Him for all kinds of things, because they are full of desires—name, fame, wealth, position and so on. They will say, "O Virgin Mary, I will make an offering to you if I get what I want. If you are successful in granting my prayer, I will worship God and give you a part of everything." Men not so material as that, but still with no faith in God, feel inclined to know about Him. They study philosophies, read scriptures, listen to lectures, and so on. They are the inquirers. The last class are those who worship God and know Him. All these four classes of people are good, not bad. All of them worship Him.[12]

Various sorts of worship we see in this world. The sick man is very worshipful to God. ... There is the man who loses his fortune; he also prays very much, to get money. The highest worship is that of the man who loves God for God's sake.[13]

CHAPTER VIII

यं यं वापि स्मरन् भावं त्यजत्यन्ते कलेवरम् ।
तं तमेवैति कौन्तेय सदा तद्भाव भावितः ॥ ६ ॥

Remembering at the end of life, whatever object (Divine Form), one leaves the body, That (Ultimate Reality) alone is reached by him or her, O son of Kunti, (because) of one's constant thought of that object. —8. 6

When a *yogi* makes a *samyama** on his own karma, upon those impressions in his mind which are now working, and those which are just waiting to work, he knows exactly by those that are waiting when his body will fall. He knows when he will die, at what hour, even at what minute. The Hindus think very much of that knowledge or consciousness of the nearness of death, because it is taught in the Gita that the thoughts at the moment of departure are great powers in determining the next life.[1]

---

* A specific mode of concentration; for details, see Patanjali's *Yoga Sutra*s.

CHAPTER IX

मयाऽध्यक्षेण प्रकृतिः सूयते सचराचरम् ।
हेतुनाऽनेन कौन्तेय जगत् विपरिवर्तते ॥ १० ॥

By reason of my over-all power, Prakriti produces all this,
the moving and the unmoving; the world wheels round and
round, O son of Kunti, because of this. —9. 10

What then is this Purusha? It is neither intelligence nor will,
but it is the cause of all these. It is its presence that sets them
all going and combining. It does not mix with nature; it is not
intelligence, or Mahat; but the Self, the pure, is Purusha. "I am
the witness, and through my witnessing, nature is producing all
that is sentient and all that is insentient."[1]

अवजानन्ति मां मूढा मानुषीं तनुं आश्रितम् ।
परं भावं अजानन्तो मम भूतमहेश्वरम् ॥ ११ ॥

Unaware of My higher state as the great Lord of beings, fools
disregard Me, when dwelling in a human form. —9. 11

God understands human failings and becomes man to do
good to humanity: "Whenever virtue subsides and wickedness
prevails, I manifest Myself. To establish virtue, to destroy evil,
to save the good I come from *yuga* (age) to *yuga*." "Fools deride
Me who have assumed the human form, without knowing My
real nature as the Lord of the universe." Such is Shri Krishna's
declaration in the Gita on Incarnation. "When a huge tidal
wave comes," says Bhagavan Shri Ramakrishna, "all the little
brooks and ditches become full to the brim without any effort or
consciousness on their own part; so when an Incarnation comes,

a tidal wave of spirituality breaks upon the world, and people feel spirituality almost full in the air."[2]

He also says, "Fools, not knowing that I, the Omnipotent and Omnipresent God of the universe, have taken this human form, deride Me and think that cannot be." Their minds have been clouded with demoniacal ignorance, so they cannot see in Him the Lord of the universe. These great Incarnations of God are to be worshipped. Not only so, they alone can be worshipped; and on the days of their birth, and on the days when they went out of this world, we ought to pay more particular reverence to them. In worshipping Christ I would rather worship Him just as He desires; on the day of His birth I would rather worship him by fasting than by feasting—by praying. When these are thought of, these great ones, they manifest themselves in our souls, and they make us like unto them. Our whole nature changes, and we become like them.[3]

तपाम्यहमहं वर्षं निगृह्णाम्युत्सृजामि च ।
अमृतं चैव मृत्युश्च सदसच्चाहमर्जुन ॥ १९ ॥

(As sun) I give heat; I withhold and send forth rain; I am immortality and also death; being and non-being am I, O Arjuna! —9 .19

The thinker of this philosophy has been struck by the idea that one power is behind all phenomena. In our thought of God, there is human limitation, personality: with Shakti comes the idea of One Universal Power. "I stretch the bow of Rudra when He desires to kill", says Shakti. The Upanishads did not develop this thought; for Vedanta does not care for the God-idea. But in the Gita comes the significant saying to Arjuna, "I am the real, and I am the unreal. I bring good, and I bring evil."[4]

अनन्याश्चिन्तयन्तो मां ये जनाः पर्युपासते ।
तेषां नित्याभियुक्तानां योगक्षेमं वहाम्यहम् ॥ २२॥

Persons who, meditating on Me as non-separate, worship
Me through everything they do, to them, who are thus ever
zealously established in yoga, I provide what they lack and
preserve what they already have. —9. 22

Listen to an old story. A lazy tramp sauntering along the
road saw an old man sitting at the door of his house and stopped
to inquire of him the whereabouts of a certain place. "How far is
such and such a village?" he asked. The old man remained silent.
The man repeated his query several times. Still there was no
answer. Disgusted at this, the traveller turned to go away. The old
man then stood up and said, "The village of__ is only a mile from
here." "What!" said the tramp, "Why did you not speak when I
asked you before?" "Because then", said the old man, "you seemed
so halting and careless about proceeding, but now you are starting
off in good earnest, and you have a right to an answer."

Will you remember this story, my son?* Go to work, the rest
will come: "Whosoever not trusting in anything else but Me,
rests on Me, I supply him with everything he needs." This is no
dream.[5]

But today there is a dark shadow in her mind. Gopala is
frightened to go alone through the wood. Never before had she[†]
felt her widowhood, her loneliness, her poverty so bitter. For a
moment it was all dark, but she recalled to her mind what she
had heard of the eternal promise: "Those that depend on Me
giving up all other thoughts, to them I Myself carry whatever is
necessary." And she was one of the souls who could believe.[6]

---

* Referring to Alasinga Perulmal.
† Gopal's Mother, in the story narrated by Swamiji, "The Story of the
Boy Gopala". (See *Complete Works*, 5.168)

I am now going to be reconciled to my life here. All my life I have been taking every circumstance as coming from Him and calmly adapting myself to it. At first in America I was almost out of my water. I was afraid I would have to give up the accustomed way of being guided by the Lord and cater for myself—and what a horrid piece of mischief and ingratitude is that. I now clearly see that He who was guiding me on the snow tops of the Himalayas and the burning plains of India is here to help me and guide me. Glory unto Him in the highest. So I have calmly fallen into my old ways. Somebody or other gives me a shelter and food, somebody or other comes to ask me to speak about Him, and I know He sends them and mine is to obey. And then He is supplying my necessities, and His will be done! "He who rests [in] Me and gives up all other self-assertion and struggles I carry to him whatever he needs."[7]

येऽपि अन्यदेवता भक्ता यजन्ते श्रद्धयाऽन्विताः ।
तेऽपि मामेव कौन्तेय यजन्ति अविधिपूर्वकम् ॥ २३ ॥

Even those devotees, who endued with *shraddha*, worship other gods, they too worship Me alone, O son of Kunti, (but) by the wrong method. —9. 23

Later on we read what Krishna says, "Even those who worship other deities are really worshipping me." It is God incarnate whom man is worshipping. Would God be angry if you called Him by the wrong name? He would be no God at all! Can't you understand that whatever a man has in his own heart is God—even if he worships a stone? What of that![8]

पत्रं पुष्पं फलं तोयं यो मे भक्त्या प्रयच्छति ।
तदहं भक्ति उपहृतं अश्नामि प्रयतात्मनः ॥ २६ ॥

Whoever with devotion offers Me a leaf, a flower, a fruit, or water, that I accept—the devout gift of the pure-minded. —9. 26

If you are strong, take up the Vedanta philosophy and be independent. If you cannot do that, worship God; if not, worship some image. If you lack strength even to do that, do some good works without the idea of gain. Offer everything you have unto the service of the Lord. Fight on! "Leaves and water and one flower—whosoever lays anything on my altar, I receive it with equal delights."[9]

So she* bathed and dressed the image, burned incense before it, and for offering?—Oh, she was so poor!—but with tears in her eyes she remembered her husband reading from the books: "I accept with gladness even leaves and flowers, fruits and water, whatever is offered with love", and she offered: "Thou for whom the world of flowers bloom, accept my few common flowers. Thou who feedest the universe, accept my poor offerings of fruits. I am weak, I am ignorant. I do not know how to approach Thee, how to worship Thee, my God, my Cowherd, my child; let my worship be pure, my love for Thee selfless; and if there is any virtue in worship, let it be Thine, grant me only love, love that never asks for anything—'never seeks for anything but love'."[10]

यत्करोषि यदश्नासि यज्जुहोषि ददासि यत् ।
यत्तपस्यसि कौन्तेय तत्कुरुष्व मदर्पणम् ॥ २७॥

Whatever you do, whatever you eat, whatever you offer in sacrifice, whatever you give away, whatever austerity you practice, O son of Kunti, do that as an offering unto Me. —9. 27

Here are the two ways of giving up all attachment. The one is for those who do not believe in God, or in any outside help. They are left to their own devices; they have simply to work with their own will, with the powers of their mind and discrimination,

---

* Gopal's Mother, in the story narrated by Swamiji, "The Story of the Boy Gopala". (See *Complete Works*, 5.168)

saying, "I must be non-attached". For those who believe in God there is another way, which is much less difficult. They give up the fruits of work unto the Lord; they work and are never attached to the results. Whatever they see, feel, hear, or do, is for Him. For whatever good work we may do, let us not claim any praise or benefit. It is the Lord's; give up the fruits unto Him. Let us stand aside and think that we are only servants obeying the Lord, our Master, and that every impulse for action comes from Him every moment. Whatever thou worshippest, whatever thou perceivest, whatever thou doest, give up all unto Him and be at rest. Let us be at peace, perfect peace, with ourselves, and give up our whole body and mind and everything as an eternal sacrifice unto the Lord. Instead of the sacrifice of pouring oblations into the fire, perform this one great sacrifice day and night—the sacrifice of your little self.[11]

Name, fame, good deeds, "Whatever sacrifices you perform, whatever penances you undergo, whatever you eat"—surrender everything to his feet. What on earth do we want? He has given us refuge, what more do we want? *Bhakti* is verily its own reward—what else is needed?[12]

मां हि पार्थ व्यपाश्रित्य येऽपि स्युः पाप योनयः ।
स्त्रियो वैश्यास्तथा शूद्राः तेऽपि यान्ति परां गतिम् ॥ ३२॥

For, taking refuge in Me, they also, O son of Pritha, who might be of inferior birth, as well as women, *vaishya*s, as well as *shudra*s—even they attain to the supreme Goal. —9. 32

"Women, or *vaishya*s, or even *shudra*s, all reach the highest goal." Breaking the bondages of all, the chains of all, declaring liberty to all to reach the highest goal, come the words of the Gita, rolls like thunder the mighty voice of Krishna.[13]

But one defect which lay in the Advaita was its being worked out so long on the spiritual plane only, and nowhere else; now the time has come when you have to make it practical. It shall no more be a *rahasya*, a secret, it shall no more live with monks in cave and forests, and in the Himalayas; it must come down to the daily, everyday life of the people; it shall be worked out in the palace of the king, in the cave of the recluse; it shall be worked out in the cottage of the poor, by the beggar in the street, everywhere; anywhere it can be worked out. Therefore do not fear whether you are a woman or a *shudra*, for this religion is so great, says Lord Krishna, that even a little of it brings a great amount of good.[14]

CHAPTER X

तेषां सतत युक्तानां भजतां प्रीतिपूर्वकम् ।
ददामि बुद्धियोगं तं येन मां उपयान्ति ते ॥१०॥

To them, ever steadfast and serving Me with affection, I give that *buddhi-yoga* by which they come unto Me. —10. 10

"The extremely beloved is desired; by whomsoever this Atman is extremely beloved, he becomes the most beloved of the Atman. So that this beloved may attain the Atman, the Lord Himself helps. For it has been said by the Lord: 'Those who are constantly attached to Me and worship Me with love—I give that direction to their will by which they come to Me.' Therefore it is said that, to whomsoever this remembering, which is of the same form as direct perception, is very dear, because it is dear to the Object of such memory perception, he is desired by the Supreme Atman, by him the Supreme Atman is attained. This constant remembrance is denoted by the word *Bhakti*." So says Bhagavan Ramanuja in his commentary on the *sutra "athato brahma-jijnasa"*.[1]

अक्षराणां अकारोऽस्मि द्वन्द्वः सामासिकस्य च ।
अहमेवाक्षयः कालो धाताहं विश्वतोमुखः ॥ ३ ३ ॥

Of letters, I am the letter A; and *dvandva* among all compounds; I alone am the inexhaustible Time; I am the Sustainer (by dispensing the fruits of actions), and the All-formed. —10. 33

The letter A is the least differentiated of all sounds, therefore Krishna says in the Gita "I am A among the letters".[2]

यद्यद्विभूतिमत्सत्त्वं श्रीमदूर्जितमेव वा ।
तत्तदेवावगच्छ त्वं मम तेजोंऽशसम्भवम् ॥ ४१ ॥

Whatever being there is great, prosperous, or powerful, you
know that to be produced from a part of My splendour. —
10. 41

Whatever is pleasure and happiness and light in the universe
belongs to Purusha; but it is a compound, because it is Purusha
plus Prakriti. "Wherever there is any happiness, wherever there is
any bliss, there is a spark of that immortality which is God."[3]

Whenever the world goes down, the Lord comes to help it
forward; and so He does from time to time and place to place. In
another passage He speaks to this effect: Wherever thou findest
a great soul of immense power and purity struggling to raise
humanity, know that he is born of My splendour, that I am there
working through him.[4]

I will find you the answer in the words of Krishna himself:
"Whenever virtue subsides and irreligion prevails, I come down.
Again and again I come. Therefore, whenever thou seest a great
soul struggling to uplift mankind, know that I am come, and
worship."[5]

It is the same light coming through glasses of different colours.
And these little variations are necessary for purposes of adaptation.
But in the heart of everything the same truth reigns. The Lord
has declared to the Hindu in His incarnation as Krishna, "I am in
every religion as the thread through a string of pearls. Wherever
thou seest extraordinary holiness and extraordinary power raising
and purifying humanity, know thou that I am there." And what
has been the result? I challenge the world to find, throughout the
whole system of Sanskrit philosophy, any such expression as that
the Hindu alone will be saved and not others.[6]

This our sages knew, and, therefore, left it open to all Indian
people to worship such great personages, such Incarnations. Nay,
the greatest of these Incarnations goes further: "Wherever an

extraordinary spiritual power is manifested by external man, know that I am there; it is from Me that that manifestation comes."That leaves the door open for the Hindu to worship the Incarnations of all the countries in the world. The Hindu can worship any sage and any saint from any country whatsoever, and as a fact we know that we go and worship many times in the churches of the Christians, and many, many times in the Mohammedan mosques, and that is good. Why not? Ours, as I have said, is the universal religion. It is inclusive enough, it is broad enough to include all the ideals. All the ideals of religion that already exist in the world can be immediately included, and we can patiently wait for all the ideals that are to come in the future to be taken in the same fashion, embraced in the infinite arms of the religion of the Vedanta.[7]

अथवा बहुनैतेन किं ज्ञातेन तवार्जुन ।
विष्टभ्याहं इदं कृत्स्नं एकांशेन स्थितो जगत् ॥ ४२ ॥

Of what avails you to know all this diversity, O Arjuna? I exist supporting this entire universe by a portion of Myself. —10. 42

All that we see of God is only a part, just as we see only one portion of the universe, and all the rest is beyond human cognition. "I, the universal; so great am I that even this universe is but a part of Me."That is why we see God as imperfect, and do not understand Him. The only way to understand Him and the universe is to go beyond reason, beyond consciousness.[8]

CHAPTER XI

तस्मात् त्वं उत्तिष्ठ यशो लभस्व
जित्वा शत्रून् भुङ्क्ष्व राज्यं समृद्धम् ।
मयैवैते निहता: पूर्व एव
निमित्तमात्रं भव सव्यसाचिन् ॥ ३ ३ ॥

Therefore, do you arise and acquire fame. Conquer the enemies, and enjoy unrivalled dominion. Verily, by Myself have they been already slain; be you merely an instrument, O Arjuna. —11. 33

Now what is that good which is to be pursued? The good for him who desires *moksha* is one, and the good for him who wants dharma is another. This is the great truth which the Lord Shri Krishna, the revealer of the Gita, has tried therein to explain, and upon this great truth is established the *varnashrama* system and the doctrine of *svadharma* etc. of the Hindu religion … . "Therefore do thou arise and acquire fame. After conquering thy enemies, enjoy unrivalled dominion; verily, by Myself have they been already slain; be thou merely the instrument, O Savyasachin (Arjuna)." In these and similar passages in the Gita the Lord is showing the way to dharma.[1]

All the sects and societies that you see, the whole host of them, inside the country or out, he [Sri Ramakrishna] has already swallowed them all, my brother. "These have verily been killed by Myself long ago, be only the instrument, O Arjuna."[2]

मया प्रसन्नेन तवार्जुनेदं
रूपं परं दर्शितमात्मयोगात् ।
तेजोमयं विश्वं अनन्तं आद्यं
यन्मे त्वदन्येन न दृष्टपूर्वम् ॥ ४७ ॥

Graciously have I shown to you, O Arjuna, this Form supreme, by My own yoga power, this resplendent, primeval, infinite, universal Form of Mine, which hath not been seen before by anyone else. —11. 47

He who believes not, believes not even after seeing, and thinks that it is all hallucination, or dream and so on. The great transfiguration of Krishna—the *Vishvarupa* (form universal)— was seen alike by Duryodhana and by Arjuna. But only Arjuna believed, while Duryodhana took it to be magic! Unless He makes us understand, nothing can be stated or understood. Somebody comes to the fullest faith even without seeing or hearing, while somebody else remains plunged in doubt even after witnessing with his own eyes various extraordinary powers for twelve years! The secret of it all is His grace! But then one must persevere, so that the grace may be received.[3]

अर्जुन उवाच –
Arjuna said:

एवं सततयुक्ता ये भक्तास्त्वां पर्युपासते ।
ये चाप्यक्षरमव्यक्तं तेषां के योगवित्तमाः ॥ १ ॥

Those devotees who, ever-steadfast, thus worship You, and those also who worship the Imperishable, the Unmanifested—which of them is better versed in yoga? —12. 1

श्री भगवान् उवाच –
The Blessed Lord said:

मय्यावेश्य मनो ये मां नित्य युक्ता उपासते ।
श्रद्धया परयोपेताः ते मे युक्ततमा मताः ॥ २ ॥

Those who, fixing their mind on Me, worship Me, ever-steadfast, and endowed with supreme *shraddha* or faith, they, in My opinion, are the best versed in yoga. —12. 2

ये तु अक्षरं अनिर्देश्यं अव्यक्तं पर्युपासते ।
सर्वत्रगं अचिन्त्यं च कूटस्थं अचलं ध्रुवम् ॥ ३ ॥

But, those who worship the Imperishable, the Indefinable, the Unmanifested, the Omnipresent, the Unthinkable, the Unchangeable, the Immovable, the Eternal. —12. 3

संनियम्येन्द्रियग्रामं सर्वत्र समबुद्धयः ।
ते प्राप्नुवन्ति मामेव सर्वभूतहिते रताः ॥ ४ ॥

Having subdued all the senses, even-minded everywhere, engaged in the welfare of all beings—verily, they reach Me only. —12. 4

क्लेशोऽधिकतरः तेषां अव्यक्तासक्त चेतसाम् ।
अव्यक्ता हि गतिर्दुःखं देहवद्भिः अवाप्यते ॥ ५ ॥

Greater is their trouble whose minds are set on the Unmanifested; for the goal of the Unmanifested is very hard to be
reached by the embodied. —12. 5

ये तु सर्वाणि कर्माणि मयि संन्यस्य मत्पराः ।
अनन्येनैव योगेन मां ध्यायन्त उपासते ॥ ६ ॥

But those who worship Me, resigning all actions in Me,
regarding Me as the Supreme Goal, meditating on Me with
single-minded yoga, —12. 6

तेषामहं समुद्धर्ता मृत्युसंसारसागरात् ।
भवामि न चिरात् पार्थ मय्यावेशित चेतसाम् ॥ ७ ॥

To these whose mind is set on Me, verily, I become ere long,
O son of Pritha, the Saviour out of the ocean of the mortal
samsara. —12. 7

[The following two paragraphs are a reference to verse 5; the
rest refer to 1 to 7.]

Here [comes] the philosopher to show us the way out, to
teach us what we really are. You may reason it out and understand
it intellectually, but there is a long way between intellectual
understanding and the practical realization of it. Between the
plan of the building and the building itself there is quite a long
distance. Therefore there must be various methods [to reach the
goal of religion]. In the last course, we have been studying the
method of philosophy, trying to bring everything under control,
once more asserting the freedom of the soul. "It is very difficult.
This way is not for [every]body. The embodied mind tries it with
great trouble."[1]

Bhakti, then, can be directed towards Brahman, only in His
personal aspect. "The way is more difficult for those whose mind

is attached to the Absolute!" *Bhakti* has to float on smoothly with the current of our nature.[2]

"Those who with constant attention always worship You, and those who worship the Undifferentiated, the Absolute, of these who are the greatest *yogis*?"—Arjuna asked of Shri Krishna. The answer was: "Those who concentrating their minds on Me worship Me with eternal constancy and are endowed with the highest faith, they are My best worshippers, they are the greatest *yogis*. Those that worship the Absolute, the Indescribable, the Undifferentiated, the Omnipresent, the Unthinkable, the All-comprehending, the Immovable, and the Eternal, by controlling the play of their organs and having the conviction of sameness in regard to all things, they also, being engaged in doing good to all beings, come to Me alone. But to those whose minds have been devoted to the unmanifested Absolute, the difficulty of the struggle along the way is much greater, for it is indeed with great difficulty that the path of the unmanifested Absolute is trodden by any embodied being. Those who, having offered up all their work unto Me, with entire reliance on Me, meditate on Me and worship Me without any attachment to anything else—them, I soon lift up from the ocean of ever-recurring births and deaths, as their mind is wholly attached to Me."

Jnana-yoga and *bhakti-yoga* are both referred to here. Both may be said to have been defined in the above passage. *Jnana-yoga* is grand; it is high philosophy; and almost every human being thinks, curiously enough, that he can surely do everything required of him by philosophy; but it is really very difficult to live truly the life of philosophy. We are often apt to run into great dangers in trying to guide our life by philosophy. This world may be said to be divided between persons of demoniacal nature who think the care-taking of the body to be the be-all and the end-all of existence, and persons of godly nature who realize that the body is simply a means to an end, an instrument intended for the culture of the soul. The devil can and indeed does cite the scriptures for his own purpose; and thus the way of knowledge appears to offer justification to what the bad man does, as much as it offers inducements to what the good man does. This is the great danger in *jnana-yoga*. But *bhakti-yoga* is natural, sweet, and gentle; the *bhakta* does not take such high flights as the *jnana-yogi*, and, therefore, he is not apt to have such big falls. Until the bondages of the soul pass away, it cannot of course be free, whatever may be the nature of the path that the religious man takes.[3]

मय्येव मन आधत्स्व मयि बुद्धिं निवेशय ।
निवसिष्यसि मय्येव अत ऊर्ध्वं न संशयः ॥ ८ ॥

Fix your mind on Me only; place your intellect in Me; then, you shall, no doubt, live in Me alone hereafter. —12. 8

Shri Krishna was God, incarnated to save mankind. *Gopi-Lila* (his disport with cowherd maids) is the acme of the religion of love in which individuality vanishes and there is communion. It is in this *Lila* that Shri Krishna shows what he preaches in the Gita: "Give up every other tie for me."[4]

अद्वेष्टा सर्व भूतानां मैत्रः करुण एव च ।
निर्ममो निरहङ्कारः सम दुःख सुखः क्षमी ॥ १३ ॥

He or she who hates no creature, and is friendly and compassionate towards all, who is free from the feelings of "I and mine", even-minded in pain and pleasure, forbearing, —12. 13

सन्तुष्टः सततं योगी यतात्मा दृढनिश्चयः ।
मय्यर्पित मनो बुद्धिः यो मद्भक्तः स मे प्रियः ॥ १४ ॥

Ever content, steady in meditation, self-controlled, and possessed of firm conviction, with mind and intellect fixed on Me—one who is thus devoted to Me, is dear to Me. —12. 14

यस्मान्नोद्विजते लोको लोकान्नोद्विजते च य: ।
हर्षामर्ष भयोद्वेगै: मुक्तो य: स च मे प्रिय: ॥ १५ ॥

One by whom the world is not agitated, and who also cannot be agitated by the world, who is freed from excessive joy, intolerance, fear and anxiety—such a one is dear to Me. — 12. 15

अनपेक्ष: शुचिर्दक्ष उदासीनो गतव्यथ: ।
सर्वारम्भ परित्यागी यो मद्भक्त: स मे प्रिय: ॥ १६ ॥

One who is free from dependence; who is pure, prompt, unconcerned, untroubled, renouncing every undertaking—one who is thus devoted to Me, is dear to Me. —12. 16

यो न हृष्यति न द्वेष्टि न शोचति न कांक्षति ।
शुभाशुभ परित्यागी भक्तिमान् य: स मे प्रिय: ॥ १७ ॥

One who neither rejoices, nor hates, nor grieves, nor desires, renouncing good and evil, full of devotion, such a one is dear to Me. —12. 17

सम: शत्रौ च मित्रे च तथा मानापमानयो: ।
शीतोष्ण सुखदु:खेषु सम: सङ्गविवर्जित: ॥ १८ ॥

One who is the sáme to friend and foe, and also in honour and dishonour, who is the same in heat and cold, and in pleasure and pain, who is free from attachment, —12. 18

तुल्यनिन्दास्तुतिर्मौनी सन्तुष्टो येन केनचित् ।
अनिकेत: स्थिरमति: भक्तिमान् मे प्रियो नर: ॥ १९ ॥

To whom censure and praise are equal, who is silent, content with anything, homeless, steady-minded, full of devotion, such a person is dear to Me. —12. 19

[The following two paragraphs are a reference to verse 13; the remaining refer to verses 13 to 19.]

Now what is that good which is to be pursued? The good for him who desires *moksha* is one, and the good for him who wants dharma is another. This is the great truth which the Lord Shri Krishna, the revealer of the Gita, has tried therein to explain, and upon this great truth is established the *varnashrama* system and the doctrine of *svadharma* etc. of the Hindu religion. "He who has no enemy, and is friendly and compassionate towards all, who is free from the feelings of 'me and mine', even-minded in pain and pleasure, and forbearing"—these and other epithets of like nature are for him whose one goal in life is *moksha*.[5]

The *sattva* prevailing, the man is inactive, he is calm, to be sure; but that inactivity is the outcome of the centralization of great powers, that calmness is the mother of tremendous energy. That highly *sattvika* man, that great soul, has no longer to work as we do with hands and feet—by his mere willing only, all his works are immediately accomplished to perfection. That man of predominating *sattva* is the Brahmin, the worshipped of all. Has he to go about from door to door, begging others to worship him? The Almighty Mother of the universe writes with Her own hand, in golden letters on his forehead, "Worship ye all, this great one, this son of Mine", and the world reads and listens to it and humbly bows down its head before him in obedience. That man is really "He who has no enemy, and is friendly and compassionate towards all, who is free from the feelings of 'me and mine', even-minded in pain and pleasure, and forbearing."[6]

"He who hates none, who is the friend of all, who is merciful to all, who has nothing of his own, who is free from egoism, who is even-minded in pain and pleasure, who is forbearing, who is always satisfied, who works always in yoga, whose self has become controlled, whose will is firm, whose mind and intellect are given up unto Me, such a one is My beloved *bhakta*. From whom comes no disturbance, who cannot be disturbed by others, who is free from joy, anger, fear, and anxiety, such a one is My beloved. He who does not depend on anything, who is pure and active, who does not care whether good comes or evil, and never becomes miserable, who has given up all efforts for himself; who is the same in praise or in blame, with a silent, thoughtful mind, blessed with what little comes in his way, homeless, for the whole world is his home, and who is steady in his ideas, such a one is My beloved *bhakta*." Such alone become *yogi*s.[7]

CHAPTER XIII

सर्वतः पाणिपादं तत् सर्वतोऽक्षिशिरोमुखम् ।
सर्वतः श्रुतिमत् लोके सर्वमावृत्य तिष्ठति ।। १३ ।।

With hands and feet everywhere, with eyes, heads, and
mouths everywhere, with ears everywhere in the universe—
That exists pervading all. —13. 13

For the whole world is one; you are rated a very insignificant
part of it, and therefore it is right for you that you should serve
your millions of brothers rather than aggrandize this little self.
"With hands and feet everywhere, with eyes, heads, and mouths
everywhere, with ears everywhere in the universe, That exists
pervading all."[1]

So give up being a slave. For the next fifty years this alone
shall be our keynote—this, our great Mother India. Let all other
vain gods disappear for the time from our minds. This is the
only god that is awake, our own race—"everywhere his hands,
everywhere his feet, everywhere his ears, he covers everything."
All other gods are sleeping. What vain gods shall we go after and
yet cannot worship the god that we see all round us, the Virat?
When we have worshipped this, we shall be able to worship all
the other gods.[2]

समं सर्वेषु भूतेषु तिष्ठन्तं परमेश्वरम् ।
विनश्यत्सु अविनश्यन्तं यः पश्यति स पश्यति ।। २७ ।।

He or she (really) sees, who sees the Supreme Lord existing
equally in all beings, the imperishable in the perishable. —
13. 27

समं पश्यन्हि सर्वत्र समवस्थितं ईश्वरम् ।
न हिनस्ति आत्मनात्मानं ततो याति परां गतिम् ॥ २८ ॥

Seeing the Lord equally present everywhere, he or she injures not the Self by the self, and so goes to the highest Goal. —13. 28

[The following paragraph is a reference to verses 27 and 28; the remaining refer to verse 28.]

Ay, if there is anything in the Gita that I like, it is these two verses, coming out strong as the very gist, the very essence, of Krishna's teaching—"He who sees the Supreme Lord dwelling alike in all beings, the Imperishable in things that perish, he sees indeed. For seeing the Lord as the same, everywhere present, he does not destroy the Self by the Self, and thus he goes to the highest goal." Thus there is a great opening for the Vedanta to do beneficent work both here and elsewhere. This wonderful idea of the sameness and omnipresence of the Supreme Soul has to be preached for the amelioration and elevation of the human race here as elsewhere. Wherever there is evil and wherever there is ignorance and want of knowledge, I have found out by experience that all evil comes, as our scriptures say, relying upon differences, and that all good comes from faith in equality, in the underlying sameness and oneness of things. This is the great Vedantic ideal.[3]

"Thus seeing the same Lord equally present everywhere, the sage does not injure the Self by the self, and thus reaches the highest goal."[4]

This is the bane of human nature, the curse upon mankind, the root of all misery—this inequality. This is the source of all bondage, physical, mental, and spiritual. "Since seeing the Lord equally existent everywhere, he injures not Self by self, and so goes to the Highest Goal." This one saying contains, in a few words, the universal way to salvation.[5]

Why do you fear to weep? Weep! Weeping clears the eyes and brings about intuition. Then the vision of diversity—man, animal, tree—slowly melting away, makes room for the infinite realization of Brahman everywhere and in every thing. Then "Verily, seeing the same God equally existent everywhere, he does not injure the Self by the self, and so goes to the Supreme Goal".[6]

Therefore the absolute sameness of conditions, if that be the aim of ethics, appears to be impossible. That all men should be the same, could never be, however we might try. Men will be born differentiated; some will have more power than others; some will have natural capacities, others not; some will have perfect bodies, others not. We can never stop that. At the same time ring in our ears the wonderful words of morality proclaimed by various teachers: "Thus, seeing the same God equally present in all, the sage does not injure Self by the self, and thus reaches the highest goal. Even in this life they have conquered relative existence whose minds are firmly fixed on this sameness; for God is pure, and God is the same to all. Therefore such are said to be living in God." We cannot deny that this is the real idea; yet at the same time comes the difficulty that the sameness as regards external forms and position can never be attained.[7]

But yet, at the same time, even the idea of the body disappears where the mind itself becomes finer and finer, till it has almost disappeared, when all the different things that make us fear, make us weak, and bind us down to this body-life have disappeared. Then and then alone one finds out the truth of that grand old teaching. What is the teaching? "Even in this life they have conquered the round of birth and death whose minds are firm-fixed on the sameness of everything, for God is pure and the same to all, and therefore such are said to be living in God." "Thus seeing the Lord the same everywhere, he, the sage, does not hurt the Self by the self, and so goes to the highest goal."[8]

Advaita and Advaita alone explains morality. Every religion preaches that the essence of all morality is to do good to others. And why? Be unselfish. And why should I? Some God has said it? He is not for me. Some texts have declared it? Let them; that is nothing to me; let them all tell it. And if they do, what is it to me? Each one for himself, and somebody take the hindermost— that is all the morality in the world, at least with many. What is the reason that I should be moral? You cannot explain it except when you come to know the truth as given in the Gita: "He who sees everyone in himself, and himself in everyone, thus seeing the same God living in all, he, the sage, no more kills the Self by the self." Know through Advaita that whomsoever you hurt, you hurt yourself; they are all you. Whether you know it or not, through all hands you work, through all feet you move, you are the king enjoying in the palace, you are the beggar leading that miserable existence in the street; you are in the ignorant as well as in the learned, you are in the man who is weak, and you are in the strong; know this and be sympathetic. And that is why we must not hurt others. That is why I do not even care whether I have to starve, because there will be millions of mouths eating at the same time, and they are all mine. Therefore I should not care what becomes of me and mine, for the whole universe is mine, I am enjoying all the bliss at the same time; and who can kill me or the universe? Herein is morality. Here, in Advaita alone, is morality explained. The others teach it, but cannot give you its reason. Then, so far about explanation.[9]

Those who have attained sameness are said to be living in God. All hatred is killing the "Self by the self", therefore love is the law of life.[10]

CHAPTER XIV

तत्र सत्त्वं निर्मलत्वात् प्रकाशकं अनामयम् ।
सुखसङ्गेन बध्नाति ज्ञानसङ्गेन चानघ ॥ ६ ॥

Of these, O sinless one, *sattva*, because of being pure, is luminous and harmless; it binds by attachment to happiness and by attachment to knowledge. —14. 6

रजो रागात्मकं विद्धि तृष्णा सङ्ग समुद्भवम् ।
तन्निबध्नाति कौन्तेय कर्मसङ्गेन देहिनम् ॥ ७ ॥

Know *rajas* to be of the nature of passion, giving rise to thirst and attachment; it binds fast, O son of Kunti, the embodied one, by attachment to action. —14. 7

तमस्तु अज्ञानजं विद्धि मोहनं सर्वदेहिनाम् ।
प्रमाद आलस्य निद्राभिः तन्निबध्नाति भारत ॥ ८ ॥

And know *tamas* to be born of ignorance, stupefying all embodied beings; it binds fast, O descendant of Bharata, by miscomprehension, indolence, and sleep. —14. 8

सत्त्वं सुखे सञ्जयति रजः कर्मणि भारत ।
ज्ञानमावृत्य तु तमः प्रमादे सञ्जयत्युत ॥ ९ ॥

Sattva makes for attachment to happiness, and *rajas* to action, O descendant of Bharata; while *tamas*, verily shrouding discrimination, attaches to miscomprehension. —14. 9

रजस्तमश्च अभिभूय सत्त्वं भवति भारत ।
रजः सत्त्वं तमश्चैव तमः सत्त्वं रजस्तथा ॥ १ ० ॥

Sattva arises, O descendant of Bharata by predominating *rajas* and *tamas*; likewise, *rajas* arises by predominating *sattva* and *tamas*; and so does *tamas* arise predominating *sattva* and *rajas.* —14. 10

With the prevalence of the *sattvika* essence, man becomes inactive and rests always in a state of deep *dhyana* or contemplation; with the prevalence of the *rajas*, he does bad as well as good works; and with the prevalence of the *tamas* again, he becomes inactive and inert. Now, tell me, looking from outside, how are we to understand, whether you are in a state wherein the *sattva* or the *tamas* prevails? Whether we are in a state of *sattvika* calmness, beyond all pleasure and pain, and past all work and activity, or whether we are in the lowest *tamasika* state, lifeless, passive, dull as dead matter, and doing no work, because there is no power in us to do it, and are, thus, silently and by degrees, getting rotten and corrupted within—I seriously ask you this question and demand an answer. Ask your own mind, and you shall know what the reality is.[1]

Sattva binds through the search for happiness and knowledge, *rajas* binds through desire, *tamas* binds through wrong perception and laziness. Conquer the two lower by *sattva*, and then give up all to the Lord and be free.[2]

CHAPTER XV

निर्मानमोहा जितसङ्गदोषा अध्यात्मनित्या विनिवृत्तकामाः ।
द्वन्द्वैर्विमुक्ताः सुखदुःखसंज्ञैर्गच्छन्त्यमूढाः पदमव्ययं तत् ॥ ५ ॥

Free from pride and delusion, with the evil of attachment
conquered, ever dwelling in the Self, with sensory desires
completely receded, liberated from the pairs of opposites
known as pleasure and pain, the undeluded reach that Goal
Eternal. —15. 5

Don't be fools always wandering from place to place; that's
all very good, but be heroes. "Free from pride and delusion, with
the evil of attachment conquered, ever dwelling in the Self, with
desires completely receded, liberated from the pairs of opposites
known as pleasure and pain, the undeluded reach that Goal
Eternal." Who advises you to jump into fire? If you don't find the
Himalayas a place for *sadhana*, go somewhere else then. So many
gushing inquiries simply betray a weak mind. Arise, ye mighty
one, and be strong! Work on and on, struggle on and on![1]

CHAPTER XVII

आयुः सत्त्व बलारोग्य सुख प्रीतिविवर्धनाः ।
रस्याः स्निग्धाः स्थिरा हृद्या आहाराः सात्त्विकप्रियाः ॥ ८ ॥

The foods which augment vitality, energy, strength, health, cheerfulness, and appetite, which are savoury and oleaginous, substantial and agreeable, are liked by the *sattvika*. —17. 8

कट्वम्ल लवणात्युष्ण तीक्ष्ण रूक्ष विदाहिनः ।
आहारा राजसस्येष्टा दुःख शोकामय प्रदाः ॥ ९ ॥

The foods that are bitter, sour, saline, excessively hot, pungent, dry, and burning, are liked by the *rajasika*, and are productive of pain, grief, and disease. —17. 9

यातयामं गतरसं पूति पर्युषितं च यत् ।
उच्छिष्टमपि चामेध्यं भोजनं तामस प्रियम् ॥ १ ० ॥

That which is stale, tasteless, stinking, cooked overnight, refuse, and impure, is the food liked by the *tamasika*. —17. 10

What the proper food is, what kind, we have to determine ourselves. Nobody can determine that [for us]. As a general practice, we have to shun exciting food. ... We do not know how to vary our diet with our occupation. We always forget that it is the food out of which we manufacture everything we have. So the amount and kind of energy that we want, the food must determine. ... The proper diet means, generally, simply do not eat highly spiced foods. There are three sorts of mind, says the *yogi*, according to the elements of nature. One is the dull mind, which covers the luminosity of the soul. Then there is that which makes people active, and lastly, that which makes them calm and peaceful. Now there are persons born with the tendency to sleep all the time. Their taste will be towards that type of food which is rotting—crawling cheese. They will eat cheese that fairly jumps off the table. It is a natural tendency with them. Then active people. Their taste is for everything hot and pungent, strong alcohol. ... *Sattvika* people are very thoughtful, quiet, and patient. They take food in small quantities, and never anything bad.[1]

दातव्यं इति यद्दानं दीयते अनुपकारिणे ।
देशे काले च पात्रे च तद्दानं सात्त्विकं स्मृतम् ॥ २० ॥

"To give is right"—gift given with this idea, to one who can do no service in return, in a fit place, time, and to a worthy person, that gift is held to be *sattvika*. —17. 20

यत्तु प्रत्युपकारार्थं फलमुद्दिश्य वा पुनः ।
दीयते च परिक्लिष्टं तद्दानं राजसं स्मृतम् ॥ २१ ॥

And what is given with a view to receiving in return, or looking for the fruit, or again reluctantly, that gift is held to be *rajasika*. —17. 21

अदेशकाले यद्दानं अपात्रेभ्यश्च दीयते ।
असत् कृतं अवज्ञातं तत् तामसं उदाहृतम् ॥ २२ ॥

The gift that is given at the wrong place or time, to unworthy persons, without regard or with disdain, that is declared to be *tamasika*. —17. 22

The Gita says that there are three kinds of charity: the *tamasika*, the *rajasika* and the *sattvika*. *Tamasika* charity is performed on an impulse. It is always making mistakes. The doer thinks of nothing but his own impulse to be kind. *Rajasika* charity is what a man does for his own glory. And *sattvika* charity is that which is given to the right person, in the right way, and at the proper time.[2]

CHAPTER XVIII

काम्यानां कर्मणां न्यासं संन्यासं कवयो विदुः ।
सर्वकर्म फलत्यागं प्राहुस्त्यागं विचक्षणाः ॥ २ ॥

The renunciation of *kamya* actions, the sages understand as *sannyasa*; the wise declare the abandonment of the fruit of all works as *tyaga*. —18. 2

Swamiji: ... No freedom without renunciation. Highest love for God can never be achieved without renunciation. Renunciation is the word—"नान्यः पन्था विद्यते अयनाय—There's no other way than this." Even the Gita says, "The sages know *sannyasa* to be the giving up of all work that has desire for its end." Nobody attains freedom without shaking off the coils of worldly worries. The very fact that somebody lives the worldly life proves that he is tied down to it as the bondslave of some craving or other. Why otherwise will he cling to that life at all? He is the slave either of lust or of gold, of position or of fame, of learning or of scholarship. It is only after freeing oneself from all this thraldom that one can get on along the way of freedom. Let people argue as loud as they please, I have got this conviction that unless all these bonds are given up, unless the monastic life is embraced, none is going to be saved, no attainment of *brahma-jnana* is possible.

Disciple: Do you mean, sir, that merely taking up *sannyasa* will lead one to the goal?

Swamiji: Whether the goal is attained or not is not the point before us now. But until you get out of this wheel of *samsara*, until the slavery of desire is shaken off, you can't attain either *bhakti* or *mukti*. To the knower of Brahman, supernatural powers or prosperity are mere trivialities.[1]

ब्राह्मण क्षत्रिय विशां शूद्राणां च परन्तप ।
कर्माणि प्रविभक्तानि स्वभाव प्रभवैः गुणैः ॥ ४१ ॥

Of *brahmana*s, *kshatriya*s and *vaishya*s, as also of *shudra*s, O scorcher of foes, the duties are distributed according to the *guna*s born of their own nature. —18. 41

शमो दमस्तपः शौचं क्षान्तिः आर्जवं एव च ।
ज्ञानं विज्ञानं आस्तिक्यं ब्रह्मकर्म स्वभावजम् ॥ ४२ ॥

The control of the mind and the senses, austerity, purity, forbearance, and also uprightness, knowledge, realization, belief in a hereafter—these are the ways of the *brahmana*s, born of (their own) nature. —18. 42

शौर्यं तेजो धृतिः दाक्ष्यं युद्धे च अपि अपलायनम् ।
दानं ईश्वरभावश्च क्षत्रकर्म स्वभावजम् ॥ ४३ ॥

Prowess, boldness, fortitude, capability, and also not flying away from battle, generosity and sovereignty are the qualities of the *kshatriya* type, born of (their own) nature. —18. 43

कृषिगौरक्ष्य वाणिज्यं वैश्यकर्म स्वभावजम् ।
परिचर्यात्मकं कर्म शूद्रस्यापि स्वभावजम् ॥ ४४ ॥

Agriculture, cattle-rearing, and trade are the duties of the *vaishya*s, born of (their own) nature; and action consisting of service is the duty of the *shudra*s, born of (their own) nature. —18. 44

स्वे स्वे कर्मणि अभिरतः संसिद्धिं लभते नरः ।
स्वकर्मनिरतः सिद्धिं यथा विन्दति तच्छृणु ॥ ४५ ॥

Devoted each to his or her own duty, a person attains the highest perfection; engaged in one's own duty, how a person attains perfection, hear that (from Me). —18. 45

The *Bhagavad Gita* frequently alludes to duties dependent upon birth and position in life. Birth and position in life and in society largely determine the mental and moral attitude of individuals towards the various activities of life. It is therefore our duty to do that work which will exalt and ennoble us in accordance with the ideals and activities of the society in which we are born.[2]

सहजं कर्म कौन्तेय सदोषं अपि न त्यजेत् ।
सर्वारम्भा हि दोषेण धूमेन अग्निः इव आवृताः ॥ ४८ ॥

One should not relinquish, O son of Kunti, the duty to which one is born, though it is attended with evil; for all undertakings are certainly enveloped by some evil, as fire by smoke. —18. 48

We find that Krishna's message has also a place for us. Without that message, we cannot move at all. We cannot conscientiously and with peace, joy, and happiness, take up any duty of our lives without listening to the message of Krishna: "Be not afraid even if there is evil in your work, for there is no work which has no evil." "Leave it unto the Lord, and do not look for the results."[3]

The result of every work is mixed with good and evil. There is no good work that has not a touch of evil in it. Like smoke round the fire, some evil always clings to work. We should engage in such works as bring the largest amount of good and the smallest measure of evil. Arjuna killed Bhishma and Drona; if this had not been done Duryodhana could not have been conquered, the force of evil would have triumphed over the force of good, and thus a great calamity would have fallen on the country. The government of the country would have been usurped by a body of proud unrighteous kings, to the great misfortune of the people. Similarly, Shri Krishna killed Kamsa, Jarasandha, and others who were tyrants, but not a single one of his deeds was done for himself. Every one of them was for the good of others. We are reading the Gita by candle-light, but numbers of insects are being burnt to death. Thus it is seen that some evil clings to work.[4]

Of course, work is always mixed with good and evil, and to work, one has to incur sin, more or less. But what of that? Let it be so. Is not something better than nothing? Is not insufficient food better than going without any? Is not doing work, though mixed with good and evil, better than doing nothing and passing an idle and inactive life, and being like stones? The cow never tells a lie, and the stone never steals, but, nevertheless, the cow remains a cow and the stone a stone. Man steals and man tells lies, and again it is man that becomes a god.[5]

The scriptures of different religions point out different means to attain the ideals of universal love, freedom, manliness, and selfless benevolence. Every religious sect is generally at variance as to its idea of what is virtue and what is vice, and fights with others over the means of attaining virtue and eschewing vice, instead of aiming at realizing the end. Every means is helpful more or less, and the Gita says, "Every undertaking is attended with defects as fire with smoke"; so the means will no doubt appear more or less defective. But as we are to attain the highest virtue through the means laid down in our respective scriptures, we should try our best to follow them. Moreover, they should be tempered with reason and discrimination. Thus, as we progress, the riddle of virtue and vice will be solved by itself.[6]

In every country, nations have their good and bad sides. Ours is to do good works in our lives and hold an example before others. No work succeeds by condemnation. It only repels people. Let anybody say what he likes, don't contradict him. In this world of Maya, whatever work you will take up will be attended with some defect. "All works are covered with defects as fire is with smoke." Every fire has a chance of being attended with smoke. But will you, on that account, sit inactive? As far as you can, you must go on doing good work.[7]

Disciple: But, sir, with the spread of learning among them*, they too will in course of time have fertile brains but become idle and inactive like us and live on the fruits of the labour of the next lower classes.

Swamiji: Why shall it be so? Even with the awakening of knowledge, the potter will remain a potter, the fisherman a fisherman, the peasant a peasant. Why should they leave their hereditary calling? "Don't give up the work to which you were born, even if it be attended with defects." If they are taught in this way, why should they give up their respective callings? Rather they will apply their knowledge to the better performance of the work to which they have been born. A number of geniuses are sure to arise from among them in the course of time.[8]

ईश्वरः सर्वभूतानां हृद्देशेऽर्जुन तिष्ठति ।
भ्रामयन् सर्वभूतानि यन्त्रारूढानि मायया ॥ ६ १ ॥

The Supreme Lord, O Arjuna, dwells in the hearts of all beings, causing all beings, by His Maya, to revolve, (as if) mounted on a machine. —18. 61

तमेव शरणं गच्छ सर्वभावेन भारत ।
तत्प्रसादात् परां शान्तिं स्थानं प्राप्स्यसि शाश्वतम् ॥ ६ २ ॥

Take refuge in Him alone with all your heart, O Bharata; by His grace you shall attain supreme peace (and) the eternal abode. —18. 62

If you are strong, take up the Vedanta philosophy and be independent. If you cannot do that, worship God; if not, worship some image. If you lack strength even to do that, do some good works without the idea of gain. Offer everything you have unto the service of the Lord. Fight on! "Leaves and water and one flower—whosoever lays anything on my altar, I receive it with

_____

* The masses.

equal delights." If you cannot do anything, not a single good work, then take refuge [in the Lord]. "The Lord resides within the heart of the being, making them turn upon His wheel. Do thou with all thy soul and heart take refuge in Him."[9]

सर्वधर्मान् परित्यज्य मामेकं शरणं व्रज ।
अहं त्वा सर्वपापेभ्यो मोक्षयिष्यामि मा शुचः ॥ ६ ६ ॥

Relinquishing all dharmas take refuge in Me alone; I will liberate you from all sins; grieve not. —18. 66

Do you think there is only a dark cup of poison if man goes to look for nectar? The nectar is there and is for every man who strives to reach it. The Lord Himself tells us, "Give up all these paths and struggles. Do thou take refuge in Me. I will take thee to the other shore, be not afraid." We hear that from all the scriptures of the world that come to us.[10]

All wise men think alike. The reader, while reading this book [*The Imitation of Christ*], will hear the echo of the *Bhagavad Gita* over and over again. Like the *Bhagavad Gita* it says, "Give up all dharmas and follow Me".[11]

I am trying to give up all anxiety unto the Lord. I am only a worker. My mission is to obey and work. He knows the rest. "Giving up all vexations and paths, do thou take refuge unto Me. I will save you from all dangers". I am trying hard to realize that. May I be able to do it soon.

Ever your affectionate brother, Vivekananda.[12]

APPENDIX

GENERAL REMARKS ON THE GITA

Even the Gita, the great philosophy itself, does not compare with that madness [of the gopis of Vrindavan], for in the Gita the disciple is taught slowly how to walk towards the goal, but here is the madness of enjoyment, the drunkenness of love, where disciples and teachers and teachings and books and all these things have become one; even the ideas of fear, and God, and heaven—everything has been thrown away.[1]

The Aryans came into India in small companies. Gradually, these tribes began to extend, until, at last, they became the undisputed rulers of India, and then arose this fight to gain the mastery, between two branches of the same family. Those of you who have studied the Gita know how the book opens with a description of the battlefield, with two armies arrayed one against the other. That is the war of the *Mahabharata*.[2]

Even the grand truths of the Gita, so boldly preached by Shri Krishna, received the gloss of compromise in the hands of future generations of disciples, and the result is that the grandest scripture of the world is now made to yield many things which lead men astray.[3]

Throughout the Gita he* is not favourable to Vedic ritual.[4]

Q.: Why, what is the defect in the present university system?

Swamiji: It is almost wholly one of defects. Why, it is nothing but a perfect machine for turning out clerks. I would even thank my stars if that were all. But no! See how men are becoming

---

* Krishna.

destitute of *shraddha* and faith. They assert that the Gita is only an interpolation, and that the Vedas are but rustic songs![5]

It [the Gita] is about five thousand years old.[6]

REFERENCES TO THE GITA VERSES

(Gita, 2.7)*

At your feet are laid a hundred and one faults of mine—"I am as thy son, so guide me who have taken refuge in thee".[7]

(Gita, 2.17)†

"None has power to destroy the unchangeable."[8]

(Gita, 2.62)

Some time ago, in a book named, *Residence in India,* written by a well-known Anglo-Indian officer, I came across such a chapter as "Native Zenana Secrets". Perhaps because of that strong desire in every human heart for knowledge of secrets, I read the chapter, but only to find that this big Anglo-Indian author is fully bent upon satisfying the intense curiosity of his own countrymen regarding the mystery of a native's life by describing an *affaire d'amour,* said to have transpired between his sweeper, the sweeper's wife, and her paramour! And from the cordial reception given to the book by the Anglo-Indian community, it seems the writer's object has been gained, and he feels himself quite satisfied with his work. "Godspeed to you, dear friends!"—What else shall we say? Well has the Lord said in the Gita: "Thinking of objects, attachment to them is formed in a man. From attachment longing, and from longing anger grows." Let such irrelevant things alone.[9]

---

* Swami Vivekananda quoted the last half of this verse in a letter to Sri Pramadas Mitra.
† With this line Swamiji opened his article on "Is the Soul Immortal", published in *The New York Morning Advertiser.*

(Gita, 2.72)*

The house which is built on a rock of ages cannot shake. I thoroughly believe that a good, unselfish and holy man like you, whose whole life has been devoted to doing good to others, has already reached this basis of firmness which the Lord Himself has styled as "rest upon Brahman" in the Gita.[10]

(Gita, 3.24)

Then what was the cause of India's downfall?—the giving up of this idea of caste. As Gita says, with the extinction of caste the world will be destroyed. Now does it seem true that with the stoppage of these variations the world will be destroyed? The present caste is not the real *jati*, but a hindrance to its progress. It really has prevented the free action of *jati*, i.e. caste or variation. Any crystallized custom or privilege or hereditary class in any shape really prevents caste (*jati*) from having its full sway; and whenever any nation ceases to produce this immense variety, it must die. Therefore what I have to tell you, my countrymen, is this, that India fell because you prevented and abolished caste.[11]

(Gita, 3.26)

Go through all the Upanishads, and even in the Samhitas, nowhere you will find the limited ideas of *moksha* which every other religion has. As to toleration, it is everywhere, even in the Samhita of the *Adhvarya Veda*, in the third or fourth verse of the fortieth chapter, if my memory does not fail; it begins with न बुद्धि भेदं जनयेदज्ञानां कर्मसंगिनाम्.† This is running through everywhere. Was anybody persecuted in India for choosing his *ishta devata*, or becoming an atheist or agnostic even, so long as he obeyed the social regulations? Society may punish anybody by its disappro-

---

* Swamiji wrote this in a letter to Haridas Viharidas Desai.
† This quotation matches with the first half of Gita, 3.36.

bation for breaking any of its regulations, but no man, the lowest *patita* (fallen), is ever shut out from *moksha*.[12]

(Gita, 4.11)

"None, O Arjuna, can swerve from my path." We are fools, and our paths are foolish. We have to go through all this Maya. God made the heaven, and man made the hell for himself.[13]

(Gita, 5.19)

Differentiation creates; homogeneity or sameness is God. Get beyond differentiation; then you conquer life and death and reach eternal sameness and are in God, are God.[14]

(Gita, 5.23)

"He who can stem the tide of lust and anger is a great *yogi*."[15]

(Gita, 6.20)

The books say that he alone is the *yogi* who, after long practice in self-concentration, has attained to this truth. The *sushumna* now opens and a current which never before entered into this new passage will find its way into it, and gradually ascend to (what we call in figurative language) the different lotus centres, till at last it reaches the brain. Then the *yogi* becomes conscious of what he really is, God Himself.[16]

(Gita, 9.19 & 10.4-5)

Very soon in the Gita we find, "O Arjuna, I am the *sat* and I am the *asat*, I am the good and I am the bad, I am the power of saints, I am the power of the wicked." But soon the speaker patches up truth, and the idea goes to sleep. I am power in good so long as it is doing good works.[17]

(Gita, 10.41)

"I am the holiness of the holy." I am the root, each uses it in his own way, but all is I. "I do everything, you are but the occasion."[18]

(Gita, 15.1, 3)

The tables have been turned, and the Hindu, who saw through tears of despair his ancient homestead covered with incendiary fire, ignited by unfriendly hands, now sees, when the searchlight of modern thought has dispersed the smoke, that his home is the one that is standing in all its strength, and all the rest have either vanished or are building their houses anew after the Hindu plan. He has wiped away his tears, and has found that the axe that tried to cut down to the roots the ऊर्ध्वमूलमध:शाखमश्वथं प्राहुरव्ययम् has proved the merciful knife of the surgeon.[19]

(Gita, 18.66)

The Lord has declared unto Arjuna: "Take thou refuge in Me, thou hast nothing else to do. And I shall deliver thee." Bholachand is mighty glad to hear this from some people; he now and then yells out in a trenchant note: "I have taken refuge in the Lord. I shall not have to do anything further." Bholachand is under the impression that it is the height of devotion to bawl out those words repeatedly in the harshest tone possible. Moreover, he does not fail to make it known now and then in the aforesaid pitch that he is ever ready to lay down his life even, for the Lord's sake, and that if the Lord does not voluntarily surrender Himself to this tie of devotion, everything would be hollow and false. And a few foolish satellites of his also share the same opinion. But Bholachand is not prepared to give up a single piece of wickedness for the sake of the Lord. Well, is the Lord really such a fool? Why, this is not enough to hoodwink us even![20]

REFERENCES

The reference (4.102-06) means: the fourth volume of *The Complete Works of Swami Vivekananda*, pages 102 to 106; similarly with the rest.

Introduction

1.	(4.102-06)	23.	(3.256)	45.	(1.87)
2.	(5.247)	24.	(4.133)	46.	(3.156)
3.	(4.428)	25.	(7.199-200)	47.	(4.106)
4.	(1.446)	26.	(6.458)	48.	(3.50)
5.	(2.292)	27.	(5.388)	49.	(4.128-29)
6.	(7.57)	28.	(9.370)	50.	(6.123)
7.	(3.244-45)	29.	(3.242)	51.	(8.8-9)
8.	(3.261)	30.	(7.185)	52.	(7.19)
9.	(6.394)	31.	(8.263)	53.	(8.227)
10.	(9.274)	32.	(9.281)	54.	(4.95)
11.	(9.370)	33.	(4.107)	55.	(5.453-54)
12.	(1.446)	34.	(1.439)	56.	(8.96)
13.	(4.106)	35.	(8.209)	57.	(4.349)
14.	(2.189)	36.	(4.106-07)	58.	(7.22)
15.	(3.396)	37.	(5.246)	59.	(6.436)
16.	(4.334-35)	38.	(4.325)	60.	(8.280)
17.	(3.328)	39.	(6.160-61)		
18.	(7.301)	40.	(1.455-56)	**Chapter I**	
19.	(5.130)	41.	(4.359)		
20.	(9.276)	42.	(4.128)	1.	(1.459)
21.	(1.444)	43.	(4.106-07)	2.	(5.416)
22.	(6.120)	44.	(5.247-48)		

Chapter II

1. (4.107-10)
2. (5.450-51)
3. (1.459-60)
4. (1.38-39)
5. (5.452-53)
6. (1.460)
7. (8.227)
8. (1.460)
9. (1.319)
10. (1.460-61)
11. (1.87-88)
12. (4.256)
13. (6.56)
14. (1.494)
15. (5.281)
16. (1.9 & 9.510)
17. (3.406)
18. (4.244)
19. (3.244)
20. (3.224)
21. (1.141)
22. (1.462)
23. (1.462)
24. (6.320)
25. (9.294)
26. (1.462)
27. (7.146)
28. (1.462)
29. (7.488)
30. (1.462)
31. (1.462)
32. (3.263)
33. (3.427)
34. (4.484)
35. (3.177)
36. (1.462-63)
37. (1.463)
38. (2.449)
39. (6.82)
40. (1.33-34)
41. (1.116)
42. (7.19)
43. (1.443)
44. (4.159)
45. (7.20)
46. (6.83-84)
47. (3.275)
48. (8.484)
49. (5.15)
50. (4.278)
51. (3.247)
52. (5.57)
53. (3.213)
54. (1.31)
55. (1.463-64)
56. (2.449)
57. (1.464)
58. (1.464-65)
59. (1.55)
60. (1.465)
61. (9.299)
62. (9.299)
63. (9.298-99)
64. (1.465-66)
65. (6.258)
66. (6.124)
67. (1.466)

Chapter III

1. (1.467)
2. (1.98)
3. (4.130)
4. (1.467)
5. (8.504)
6. (3.236)
7. (1.106)
8. (1.98)
9. (5.249)
10. (7.179)
11. (2.1-2)
12. (2.2-3)
13. (1.467)
14. (7.14)
15. (1.441)
16. (1.58)
17. (1.467)
18. (3.122-23)
19. (5.456)
20. (1.467-68)
21. (5.455)
22. (5.309)
23. (5.263-64)
24. (1.470)
25. (1.468)
26. (1.471)
27. (1.236)
28. (5.248)
29. (1.472)
30. (1.451-52)
31. (1.473)
32. (1.474)
33. (1.41)
34. (1.474)

Chapter IV

1. (1.474-75)
2. (4.257)
3. (1.475)
4. (4.151-52)
5. (1.444-45)
6. (1.475)
7. (1.484)
8. (3.55-56)

9. (4.31)
10. (4.154)
11. (4.321)
12. (3.250)
13. (8.209-10)
14. (3.138)
15. (3.313)
16. (1.444)
17. (4.95)
18. (3.304)
19. (1.4 & 9.430)
20. (1.475)
21. (6.169)
22. (1.440)
23. (8.49)
24. (6.271-72)
25. (1.476)
26. (6.327)
27. (7.179-80)
28. (1.457)
29. (2.292-93)
30. (1.476)
31. (1.34)
32. (4.96)
33. (1.442-43)
34. (4.131)
35. (4.286-87)
36. (7.271-73)
37. (1.476)
38. (1.477)
39. (1.477)
40. (4.343-44)
41. (7.197-98)
42. (7.257)
43. (5.132-33)
44. (7.240)
45. (4.483-84)

Chapter V

1. (8.383-84)
2. (1.93)
3. (4.130)
4. (1.12)
5. (3.10)
6. (1.60)
7. (1.101)
8. (7.178-79)
9. (1.53)
10. (1.425)
11. (5.285)
12. (6.150)
13. (3.263)
14. (1.425-26)
15. (1.434-35)
16. (3.349)
17. (3.433)
18. (4.328-29)
19. (5.305)
20. (8.344)

Chapter VI

1. (8.251)
2. (6.273)
3. (1.478)
4. (2.403)
5. (8.132)
6. (5.146-47)
7. (6.427)
8. (5.47-48)
9. (6.227-28)
10. (1.136)
11. (1.518)
12. (6.130)
13. (8.16)
14. (6.283)

15. (3.425)
16. (6.83)
17. (7.64)
18. (3.66-67)
19. (7.195)
20. (7.237)
21. (5.55)
22. (5.382)
23. (7.160-61)
24. (6.415)
·25. (2.36)
26. (6.483)

Chapter VII

1. (2.248)
2. (8.384)
3. (1.18)
4. (2.381)
5. (3.262)
6. (3.476)
7. (2.106-07)
8. (2.123)
9. (1.497)
10. (9.293)
11. (9.268)
12. (8.119-20)
13. (1.440)

Chapter VIII

1. (1.278)

Chapter IX

1. (2.451)
2. (3.55-56)
3. (4.31-32)
4. (8.253)

5. (5.60)
6. (6.171)
7. (7.454)
8. (1.468)
9. (1.443)
10. (6.170)
11. (1.102)
12. (6.346)
13. (3.263)
14. (3.427)

Chapter X

1. (3.35)
2. (3.58)
3. (2.451)
4. (4.152)
5. (1.444)
6. (1.18)
7. (3.251-52)
8. (2.449)

Chapter XI

1. (5.450-51)
2. (6.346)
3. (6.481)

Chapter XII

1. (1.504)
2. (3.42)
3. (3.77-78)
4. (6.110-11)
5. (5.450)
6. (5.451-52)
7. (1.193)

Chapter XIII

1. (3.446-47)
2. (3.300-01)
3. (3.193-94)
4. (3.263)
5. (4.329)
6. (4.492)
7. (1.434-35)
8. (3.349)
9. (3.425)
10. (7.31)

Chapter XIV

1. (5.451)
2. (7.81)

Chapter XV

1. (6.243-44)

Chapter XVII

1. (1.518-19)
2. (9.418)

Chapter XVIII

1. (6.505)
2. (1.64)
3. (4.132)
4. (5.248-49)
5. (5.451)
6. (5.420)
7. (7.221)
8. (7.149-50)

9. (1.443)
10. (1.342)
11. (8.160)
12. (8.501)

Appendix

1. (3.259)
2. (4.78-79)
3. (5.264)
4. (5.322)
5. (5.364-65)
6. (9.276)
7. (6.224)
8. (4.253)
9. (4.410)
10. (8.296)
11. (4.372)
12. (4.341-42)
13. (1.476)
14. (7.18)
15. (7.64)
16. (2.35-36)
17. (6.147)
18. (7.81)
19. (4.349)
20. (6.192)

INDEX

CW = *The Complete Works of Swami Vivekananda* (Vol & page/s).
G = Bhagavad Gita (Chapter & verse/s).
Intro. = "Introduction" of this book.
* = This particular quotation is placed in the "Appendix".
App. = "Appendix" of this book.

CW	G	CW	G	CW	G
7.178-79	5.11	8.49	4.11	8.384	7.3*
7.179	3.19	8.71	5.10	8.484	2.47
7.179-80	4.17*	8.96	Intro.	8.501	18.66
7.185	Intro.	8.119-20	7.16	8.504	3.17
7.195	6.35	8.132	6.5	9.268	7.16
7.197-98	4.33	8.160	18.66	9.274	Intro.
7.199-200	Intro.	8.209-210	4.7-8	9.276	App.
7.221	18.48	8.209	Intro.	9.281	Intro.
7.237	6.40	8.227	2.11	9.293	7.14
7.240	4.38	8.227	Intro.	9.294	2.29
7.257	4.34*	8.251	6.5	9.298-99	2.67
7.271-73	4.18	8.253	9.19	9.299	2.60
7.301	Intro.	8.263	Intro.	9.299	2.62-63
7.454	9.22	8.280	Intro.	9.370	Intro.
7.488	2.38	8.296	2.72	9.418	17.20-22*
8.8-9	Intro.	8.344	5.19	9.430	4.11
8.16	6.16	8.383-84	5.3	9.510	2.23-24